SEVEN
LEVERS

Praise for *Seven Levers*

"This book is gold in terms of immediate potential to help many United Methodist conferences finally shift from a perpetual sea of logjams into liberation for mission. In fact, *Seven Levers* is itself an unprecedented lever for our denomination!"
> —Sue Nilson Kibbey, Director of Connectional and Missional Church Initiatives, West Ohio Conference (United Methodist Church)

"*Seven Levers* is an exceptionally rigorous and comprehensive rethinking of annual conference life and practice. Filled with insight, examples, provocation, and hope, it can contribute to a transformation of this basic unit of the church, which currently is living out of a model designed for another era."
> —Lovett H. Weems Jr., Director, Lewis Center for Church Leadership, Wesley Theological Seminary

"*Seven Levers* charts a clear and compelling course for annual conferences and other judicatories to transform their congregations as missional outposts. For far too long, annual conferences have managed institutional decline rather than led transformational change. *Seven Levers* gives hope to conferences ready for a new day."
> —Douglas T. Anderson, Associate Director of Church Development, Indiana Conference (United Methodist Church)

"*Seven Levers* offers an unprecedented analysis of conference operations as well as insights on how to refocus resources toward the mission. Positive and hopeful, *Seven Levers* will change your conference. I heartily recommend it for every clergy and lay member of the annual conference."
> —Janice Huie, Bishop, Texas Conference (United Methodist Church)

"Thankfully the UMC is learning much about *who* we now are and *what* we are called to do. We still must do the hard work of *how*—the rubber-on-the-road work. *Seven Levers* is important reading for leaders seeking steps forward."
> —Gil Rendle, senior consultant, the Texas Methodist Foundation, and author of *Journey in the Wilderness* and *Back to Zero*

"Robert Schnase has the gift to think strategically and systemically about the purpose of the church of Jesus Christ and its mission in our time. He identifies seven levers that have the greatest potential to move to where we might be, through the grace of God. If we are to flourish, we will need more complex and necessary innovations within our annual conferences."
> —Ken Carter, Bishop, Florida Conference (United Methodist Church)

SEVEN LEVERS

Missional Strategies for Conferences

Robert Schnase

Abingdon Press™

Nashville

SEVEN LEVERS:
MISSIONAL STRATEGIES FOR CONFERENCES

Copyright © 2014 by Robert Schnase

Library of Congress Cataloging-in-Publication Data

Schnase, Robert C., date.
  Seven levers : missional strategies for conferences / Robert Schnase.
     pages cm
  ISBN 978-1-4267-8207-7 (alk. paper)
1. Church management. 2. Church development, New. 3. United Methodist Church (U.S.) I. Title.
  BV652.S3585 2014
  287'.6—dc23

                                                                    2013048136

14 15 16 17 18 19 20 21 22 23—10 9 8 7 6 5 4 3 2 1

MANUFACTURED IN THE UNITED STATES OF AMERICA

CONTENTS

INTRODUCTION

Seven Levers: Missional Strategies for Conferences uses the image of a lever to describe fundamental strategies that work. Levers are tools that multiply the results of our effort. Using levers, we can move things that otherwise we could never budge. Levers are critical operational focal points for change in a conference that help us derive disproportionate effects. When these seven essentials work well, then other important work becomes achievable.

Seven Levers explores annual conferences in operational terms—what they do, how they work, what their limitations and possibilities are. *Seven Levers* invites us to rethink the nature and purpose of United Methodist conferences, not merely the three-day annual gathering, but the whole array of people, projects, resources, and practices that comprise our common ministry.

Seven Levers encourages leaders to think afresh. What works and what doesn't and why? How do we change approaches that are no longer conducive to our mission? What strategies foster a more relevant and effective connectionalism?

This isn't a "how to" manual, but a "what's most important" catalyst. It doesn't provide a one-size-fits-all template; rather it encourages learning, experimenting, and contextual response. It draws attention toward the mission of the church.

Seven Levers stimulates the search for strategies that give hope and direction.

A Healthier Conversation

The United Methodist Church faces extraordinary challenges—the decline in US attendance, the aging of our membership, the rising costs of sustaining ministry, the difficulty of reaching younger generations. These have stimulated experiments that no one could have anticipated a few years ago. During this time of flux, fluidity, and recalibration, the drive to remain relevant, vital, and missionally focused elicits considerable conversation about leadership.

Three approaches toward church leadership don't help.

The first is the *Ethereal Saint*. Writers, consultants, pastors or laity who take this stance say, "We just need to have faith. All is in God's hands and God will take care of us." They argue that "it's not about fruitfulness but faithfulness." Or they say, "If God wants our church to survive, it will thrive, and if not, it will die. Don't worry about decline. Trust the Holy Spirit."

This approach is fundamentally *un*carnational and denies reality. This is an avoidance tactic, naïve and irresponsible. It asks God to do for us what God created us to do for God. Rather than trusting God, it represents a breach of the trust God has placed in us. God calls us to use our gifts, creativity, and passion to fulfill God's purpose as best we can. We can't ignore or deny the challenges before us, thinking someone or something will rescue us.

The second approach is the *Technocrat*, the church leader who wholly adopts the corporate language of analysis, statistics, effectiveness, and metrics to comprehend church life, reducing everything to charts, graphs, input, and outcome. We have much to learn from the literature of leadership, and I've been a student of organizations throughout my ministry. But there are limits to what executive language can provide. These analyses presume too linear a process, too simple a connection between cause and effect, and too naïve a notion of how authority in the church is exercised. Ministry isn't an exact science, and we can't "fix" the church with technical expertise the way a mechanic replaces parts or retunes an engine. The Technocrat doesn't account for the messiness of church life, the immeasurable aspects of ministry, the inexplicable passions that knit followers of Christ to each other, the unpredictability of the Spirit, or the wild, raw nature of God. We learn from business, but the body of Christ is fundamentally not a business.

The *Doomsayer*, a third approach to leadership in the church, is the purveyor of despair, repeating the narrative of decline in weighty and punishing tones. Fostering a sense of impending calamity defeats the spirit and leads to the organizational equivalent of a panic attack that leaves people paralyzed and feeling helpless. The Doomsayer feeds our obsession with growth in the desperate struggle to survive. Fear isn't a positive motivator. Fear excites a temporary urgency, but fails to provide the basis for identity, courage, and mission. The Doomsayer doesn't leave room for the interruption of the Spirit, for unexpected and unexplained renewal, or for resurrection in times and places no one can predict.

We can do better. A healthier conversation realistically embraces the challenges we face while keeping faith in God, whose nature is life and new birth. It requires learning and experimentation, attention to the mission field, persistence, and making hard decisions about what to cast off and what to take up. Leading requires pouring ourselves into long-term tasks with patience and attending to outcomes with honesty and humility. Leading the church takes courage and passion, boldness and playfulness, and a willingness to confront each other with things we might rather avoid and to talk each other into creative new work.

Seven Levers: Missional Strategies for Conferences doesn't posit simple solutions or quick fixes and offers no magic formulas or silver bullets. It describes our current circumstances with honesty. Unlike the approach of the Ethereal Saint, this book invites us to get our hands dirty by entering the tangled complexity of conferences in order to align purposes, reconsider systems, and renew commitments to the unfathomable mission of Christ. Instead of the voice of a Technocrat or expert, the book lifts up practitioners in the field, leaders well acquainted with the oddities, limitations, and extraordinary possibilities of conferences. Rather than leaving readers with a low-grade depression (as Doomsayers do), *Seven Levers* gives permission to experiment and encourages us to draw the energy, attention, and focus of the conference toward the mission rather than toward internal structures. It stimulates imagination and challenges us to reinvent conferences. *Seven Levers* helps us set ourselves free.

How to Use the Book

Use *Seven Levers* for conversations among clergy in peer mentoring and covenant groups, for catalyst conversations, and at clergy retreats. Introduce the concepts to incoming clergy during residency in ministry. Cover each chapter one at a time, sharing suggestions and experiments. Engage honestly, and challenge signs of avoidance, denial, or blaming.

Invite alternative ideas. Resolve for a better, missionally focused experience of conference. Encourage one another into greater boldness in service to Christ.

Use *Seven Levers* to train laity for leadership through the board of laity, at Lay Servant Ministries events, and in the curriculum for lay ministry preparation. Help people identify, "What's our strategy in this conference for that lever?" Empower laity to lead.

Distribute the book to all members of conference who have voice and vote. *Seven Levers* provides a unifying language for articulating priorities and strategies. Encourage future-oriented conversation about your conference and how to move toward greater fruitfulness. *Seven Levers* will change your conference.

Use the Conversation Questions at the back of each chapter to guide discussions. Invite vigorous and deliberate conversation and prayerful engagement with the issues.

Seven Levers assists bishops, lay leaders, superintendents, conference staff, planning committees, and all those people who serve on conference boards, committees, foundations, and teams. Let these levers shape planning retreats, strategy sessions, and balcony conversations.

The website, SevenLevers.org, includes sample documents, handouts, outlines, evaluations, principles, and practices related to each of the levers for those who want to delve deeper.

Above all, allow *Seven Levers* to shape your own reflections about your conference and your leadership within it, your personal discipleship, and your ministry in Christ. Use the levers, amend them, and deepen them to extend the mission of Christ.

Like the laity and clergy reading this book, I'm a practitioner in leading conferences and not an expert. God has given us a task of unbelievable scope and overwhelming proportion, larger than any of us and bigger than all of us. We are also blessed with immeasurable resources, with thousands of congregations and millions of people and billions of dollars in assets and a spiritual inheritance that is indescribably vibrant and life giving. We've been assigned a mission field that begins in the neighborhood of each congregation and extends to the ends of the earth. For this, The United Methodist Church needs all the tools we can discover or create. May *Seven Levers* help us recover the incredible resource of conference to help us fulfill the mission of Christ in ever more faithful and fruitful ways.

THE COMPLEXITY OF CONFERENCES

Most people reading this book have received, experienced, observed, or led some form of ministry through conferences. All of us perceive conference operations from a particular perspective as a pastor, layperson, superintendent, or staff member, and we're aware of the great potential and serious limitations of conferences. This book is about fundamental strategies for increasing the number of fruitful congregations, improving the quality of clergy leadership, and extending the United Methodist witness in the world. It explores conferences in operational terms—how they work and what keeps them from working better. As you read this chapter, think about your own experiences. How has belonging to a conference impacted your ministry, and how have you been involved? What has frustrated you or limited your conference's ability to multiply ministry?

With few exceptions, I've found serving on conference committees frustrating, tedious, and exasperating. Much conference work is unfocused, disconnected, unfruitful, perfunctory, and redundant. I've despaired of committee work empty of purpose or ensnared by confusing policies, rules, and procedures. Most work remains completely irrelevant to the local congregation, which is the principal ministry delivery system for our mission, and equally disconnected from the real-world concerns of the people we seek to serve. I've puzzled over impenetrably complex systems for credentialing and ordination, restraints on local church initiative, and obtuse funding systems. Conferences seldom display a consistent vision, identity, or common understanding of their mission, and few have strategies for improving leadership or increasing the number of vital congregations.

1

This is not to say that I don't appreciate the positive potential of conferences. I first attended conference when I was fourteen years old. I met the young woman who would become my wife at a conference youth retreat. The heroes of my young adulthood were the pastors, laypersons, and youth directors who influenced my call to ministry at conference events. For twenty-five years, I served on conference committees and boards, and sometimes we accomplished significant work. As a bishop, I've come to know the inner workings of conferences, and I've seen the fruit of focused effort. As a writer and speaker, I've visited more than thirty US conferences as well as conferences in Africa, Europe, Asia, and Central and South America. Conferences make a difference.

But for the most part, conferences are large, complex organizations that operate in ways that are no longer conducive to our mission. They remain an underutilized resource because they are poorly focused, are diffuse in purpose, and operate with inadequate systems of accountability and poor alignment of time, personnel, and resources.

Members of conferences sense something is wrong, as evidenced by constant calls to restructure, change job descriptions, and reduce costs. Current operations produce frustrated bishops, burned-out superintendents, underappreciated staff, detached pastors, and exasperated laypersons.

An unstated notion that "churches exist to serve conferences" drives many conversations and feeds much cynicism. Churches feel burdened by apportionments and weighed down by reporting processes. People love the relationships fostered by belonging to conference but feel exasperated by the lack of identifiable, fruitful outcomes for their work. Conferences haven't done well in establishing and reinforcing a missional urgency, other than that created by the fear of decline. Most conferences don't have a sufficient coalition of leaders focused on the mission to foster change and alignment. Leaders operate with unclear priorities in an environment rich with distractions, marked by conflict, and hampered by competing demands for attention, which limit the ability to give sustained focus toward the challenges that most require our work.

All the Moving Parts

What is a United Methodist annual conference? I'm not referring merely to the three-day annual meeting of clergy and lay delegates. Rather, what are the components that a conference likely comprises, and how do all the moving parts work together?

Take a moment to think about your annual conference. Name as many of the constituent parts, bodies, organizations, units, agencies, and ministries as you can. Begin with the number of congregations, members, and clergy, including full-time, part-time, and retired. For instance, I serve the Missouri Conference, comprised in 2013 of 855 congregations with 997 active and retired clergy and 165,000 members who worship in properties valued at $1.2 billion. The conference operates on a $14 million budget, and gives $1.3 million each year to Advance Specials and $1.1 million to other UM causes.

Then think about the bishop, the episcopal staff, offices, and residence. Move to the cabinet, the superintendents, the districts, their offices. A conference like my own has twelve districts that operate with their own staff and property. Next, walk through the conference office in your imagination, greeting the people who work on pensions, health insurance, pastoral records. Continue through the treasurer's office, thinking of apportionments, missional giving, property management, and the conference journal. Move to those who supervise new church starts or lead clergy recruitment or who do communications, including websites, newsletters, mailings, logos, and so on. Don't forget those who work with camping and retreat ministries, their employees and property (in our case, four camps), or those responsible for children and youth ministries and safe sanctuaries policies. Perhaps your conference has trainers for disaster response teams, for Volunteers in Mission, or for social justice ministries.

The conference office is merely the beginning for understanding conference responsibilities. Campus ministry personnel and their facilities are scattered across the region, as are social agencies owned by or related to the conference, including colleges, universities, medical clinics, hospitals, foundations, credit unions, or ministries with refugees—all with staffs and facilities and budgets, some directly and legally extensions of the conference and others related merely by history and identity. Don't overlook the clergy training components, including the Course of Study, seminaries, scholarships, residency in ministry programs, and the district committees and mentors and psychological consultants.

Now step further out to view the work of your conference around the country and across the globe, including partnerships with conferences in Africa, Asia, or Europe; mission projects; long-term international relationships; safe water projects; and construction work far away for orphanages, schools, clinics, or churches. Some conferences have full-time staff abroad and long-standing agreements with partner conferences.

3

All of these components have directors, boards, supervisors, employees, property, budgets, policies, and constituents whom they serve. Now turn your attention to conference-wide associations such as United Methodist Women, the School of Christian Mission, United Methodist Men, Emmaus Walk, those in extension ministries, and organizations formed by common affinities such as scouting, Christian educators, church secretaries, the Reconciling Ministries Network, the Federation for Social Action, Black Methodists for Church Renewal, the Confessing Movement, and so on.

We haven't yet mentioned the actual governing mechanisms of the conference, many prescribed by the *Book of Discipline* and others created for unique contexts, including the conference council, Board of Trustees, Council on Finance and Administration, Lay Leaders Council, Board of Ordained Ministry, and the conference committees that align with general agencies, including Global Ministries, Church and Society, Higher Education and Campus Ministry, Discipleship, Religion and Race, Status and Role of Women, Communication, Ecumenical Relations, and Archives and History. This is in addition to planning annual conference sessions with thousands of people, plus dozens of other annual events for youth, pastors, and laity.

Are you overwhelmed yet? Hang in there. There are also the ministries indigenous to your own conference. In Missouri, these include the Festival of Sharing, WOW, Converge, Surge, the Mozambique Initiative, SERVE, PET, Exploration, Candidacy Summit, the Hannah Project, Pastoral Leadership Development groups, the Healthy Church Initiative, the Small Church Initiative, Haiti Safe Water project, and Lay Leadership Development groups. There are conference confirmation retreats, summer youth mission projects, and internships.

Your own conference may have similar ministries by different names. What would you add that is unique to your conference?

Simply naming a ministry on a list doesn't capture the complexity and responsibility each entails. For instance, WOW is an annual weekend gathering of 2,400 youth and sponsors. The three letters, *W-O-W*, don't convey the immensity of planning—transportation, rooms, meals, worship, guest speakers, workshops, communications, registration, costs, safe sanctuaries credentialing, or liability—that this single event involves. The same could be said for VIM—mobilizing hundreds of work teams around the world; or UMW—having twelve thousand members; or Festival of Sharing—bringing together several thousand people to serve tens of thousands in need; or SERVE—using more than twelve thousand volunteers to reach more than ninety thousand people; or safe sanctuaries—handling twenty thousand applications for people serving youth and children.

Nor does the list capture the enormous impact of a ministry. Even though they are corporately unrelated to the conference, Central Methodist University with its five thousand students and the Missouri United Methodist Foundation with its $75 million in assets extend the witness of United Methodism in remarkable ways, along with several other agencies originally established by the church.

A name on the list can't express the positive fruit when the work goes well or the massive impact if it is done poorly. Decisions about clergy insurance and pensions involve millions of dollars and hundreds of families. Safe sanctuaries, the camping and youth ministries, and the clergy supervision systems have enormous implications for keeping children safe or opening the conference to immeasurable liability.

Are you surprised by the long list of components, ministries, and infrastructure of an annual conference?

During my first year as bishop, I received a letter from someone questioning the well-being of our horses at camp. On the same day, I received a petition from residents of a retirement home expressing discontent with a policy of the institution, and another letter from a neighbor of a rural church complaining about the fireworks show held on church property. I also received a letter railing against a church cemetery association and another critical about the lack of financial support for the renovation of an athletic facility at a United Methodist–related school.

Horses? Retirement homes? Fireworks? Cemeteries? Athletic centers? How are these related? If we could white out all the references to church, bishop, and United Methodist on these five topics, could anyone possibly guess what organization links them in any way? The Missouri Conference of The United Methodist Church!

What do we learn from this exercise?

First, we badly underestimate the size and complexity of annual conferences and how difficult they are to lead, manage, direct, and coordinate. And we miscalculate how much energy each moving part requires.

Many of the components operate independently, with little relationship to the center. On the other hand, any of these can leap to the center of attention in a moment's time when conflicts emerge, or if there are personnel, financial, legal, or misconduct issues.

And each demands attention from conference leadership. Each

wonders, "What's our place, and is our voice heard? Do we matter to those in authority? What is the conference doing for us?"

Second, it's an operational misconception to think that a United Methodist conference has a perfectly efficient cascading mechanism by which to embed culture, strategy, value, vision, or practice. I wish I had a dime for every time a business leader or a pastor said, "Why don't you just make all the churches do such-and-such? Why don't you make all your pastors attend this or that event?" People presume a hierarchy in which a bishop tells the superintendents something to pass along to the pastors who then instruct their laity, and then something is completed with great efficiency. They picture the conference trustees making a decision, and then all the local trustees follow suit. That's not how things work. As one consultant quipped, "A conference is an automobile with multiple steering wheels."

Authority is diffuse in the United Methodist system. Bishops and conference governing boards lead an all-volunteer army. Local congregations are autonomous to an extraordinary degree (and we wouldn't want to change that!), and most components operate independently with separate governing and supervision systems. Think about how many different people serve in leadership and governance positions across our hundreds of congregations. Think about their diverse experiences, perceptions, aptitudes, and interests. Communication doesn't move smoothly, efficiently, or thoroughly through such a system. Mandates don't work with specific expectations (completing a form on time, for instance) and even less so with the softer qualities of vision, value, and culture. It's seldom useful to say "every church must_____" or "every pastor is required to _____."

Third, most pressures on the organization militate against streamlining, unifying, and cooperating on a common vision, mission, and set of values. Representatives on conference committees receive pressure from their constituencies to make sure their particular interest receives support. Whether someone represents camping, campus ministry, UMW, a service agency, an ethnic caucus, young people, or a ministry related to a general board, they are primed to protect and promote their interests throughout the system. This creates divided loyalties and competing claims. Change becomes difficult to achieve.

Fourth, this exercise reminds us of the vast and extensive resources available for an annual conference. And yet most conferences, even with a wealth of people and resources, are ill equipped to face the most critical challenges of our mission.

Conferences are large organizations with hundreds of moving parts comprising incredible numbers of people. They operate with multimillion-dollar budgets, oversee tens of millions in pensions, supervise hundreds of clergy, and own buildings, residences, campus ministry sites, and retreat centers worth millions. And yet most operate without a compelling, unifying vision that stimulates a sense of urgency. Most fail to mobilize clergy, laity, congregations, and institutions to reach new people, foster greater life-changing ministry, or maintain a missional focus.

Even with the sophisticated infrastructure and superstructure of all fifty-seven US conferences, and under the leadership of forty-seven bishops, more than four hundred superintendents and thousands of conference staff, The United Methodist Church continues to decline precipitously in the United States. Lovett Weems has noted that despite all the resources we employ and the six billion dollars in new money each year for the purpose of making disciples, The United Methodist Church hasn't been able to reach one more person than it started with each year, and that's been true for every year since 1966.[1]

How's That Working?

Bryce Hoffman tells the story of Ford Motor Company's CEO, Alan Mulally, when Mulally began to lead the company back to profitability after years of struggle.[2] Company executives reported each week on all the projects and portfolios under their responsibility with three color codes. Red indicated a problem area of sufficient concern that the project wouldn't proceed until issues were resolved. Yellow meant questions were arising that needed to be addressed, but the project would continue. And Green meant the project was proceeding as planned with no major issues.

For months after Mulally began as CEO, all the charts were Green. Executives talked in positive terms about how everything in their area of responsibility was proceeding as planned. Finally, Mulally interrupted the weekly reports, and said, "We're going to lose billions of dollars this year. Is there anything that's *not* going well here?"[3]

Then one week, an executive responsible for a major product release reported that they had discovered significant problems, and listed the project as Red. People sat in silence, stunned by the audacity to honestly describe the setback. The silence was broken by one person applauding— Alan Mulally, the CEO. He didn't criticize or fire the executive who dared to code Red a major project. Instead, Mulally turned to the others and invited them to get to work on how each department could help overcome the setbacks in the project.

United Methodist conferences behave similarly. We receive reports from across the connection and congratulate ourselves on our continuing good work in our individual responsibilities. How's the camping program? Outstanding. How's campus ministry going? We appointed a new person, and it's turning around. How do the Board of Ordained Ministry and the cabinet work together? Better than ever. How was annual conference this year? The worship was amazing. How's the new church start? We finally found the right pastor for the job. Apportionments? Giving is up a little. Volunteers in Mission? Disaster response? Doing amazing work. Conference youth ministry? Lay training? On track.

Everything gets the Green. Every ministry is above average. Multiply that by fifty-seven US conferences and you would think we were thriving!

If everything is going according to plan, why have we declined by over 162,000 people in worship attendance over the last four years? Think about the size and scope of the Missouri Conference as I described it earlier in the chapter. In the four years between General Conference 2012 and General Conference 2016, United Methodism in the United States will decline in attendance, membership, and numbers of churches by an equivalent to completely closing down all the ministries of *two* conferences the size of Missouri. Something isn't working right. Something isn't going according to plan.

I'm not resorting to doomsayer tactics. These are honest numbers that reveal the depth of our situation. Because we have no space to be honest and vulnerable, we duck and weave and hide about how things are going in our areas of responsibility. But our hope lies in figuring things out together.

In 2009, the Council of Bishops commissioned the most extensive, thorough, independent organizational study ever undertaken on a mainline denomination. Based on the analysis of forty years of statistics for more than thirty-three thousand United Methodist churches in the United States, plus hundreds of interviews with congregations, pastors, and laity across the connection, the 250-page Towers-Watson Report confirms patterns of precipitous decline and long-term financial unsustainability.[4]

The Towers-Watson Report identifies causes for decline, including rampant mistrust, dysfunctional decision-making processes, distance between the people in the pew and the leaders in authority, unsustainable financial models, a crisis of relevance, difficulty in recruiting clergy, the age gap between current congregations and the mission field, unclear means of viewing progress and unreliable measures of fruitfulness, too much complacency, and no clear vision, priorities, or strategies. The report calls for long-term systemic change throughout the United Methodist connection.

The Towers-Watson Report offers five recommendations that were accepted and approved by the Council of Bishops, and which became the *Call to Action*.[5]

1. *Give sustained focus on increasing the number of vital congregations* that make disciples of Jesus Christ for the transformation of the world, and align resources accordingly. This means developing more effective systems for starting congregations, reversing trends in existing congregations, strengthening drivers that correlate with vitality, and experimenting with alternative models for forming faith communities.

2. *Reform clergy systems.* Clergy systems involve recruitment, candidacy, mentoring, education, skills training, supervision, evaluation, deployment, and retirement.

3. *Streamline decision-making processes.* This includes better collaboration, greater missional alignment, and faster responsiveness to trends in the mission field.

4. *Use metrics to evaluate progress.* The report invites leaders to adopt an unapologetic focus on fruitfulness, outcomes, and accountability. If it works, teach it and multiply it. If it bears no fruit, stop doing it.

5. *Reform the Council of Bishops.* This mostly involves challenging the Council of Bishops to focus on the previous four recommendations with diligence.

The Towers-Watson Report and the *Call to Action* are positive signs. The two most critical recommendations fall within the influence of annual conferences—increasing the number of vital congregations and reforming clergy systems. The levers with the greatest impact are closest at hand and within the purview of annual conferences. That's what this book is about.

A System No One Intended

John Wesley established conferences in order to strengthen and multiply faith communities and to extend the Methodist witness. Conferences were a missional instrument, the means by which the church initiated ministry, provided streams of leadership, prepared people for the mission field, and inspired them in their work.

No one intended to create conferences so complex, diffuse, and difficult to lead. Nevertheless, we've inherited systems that are no longer conducive to our mission. They respond slowly, and the endless checks and balances foster an institutional conservatism that makes change nearly impossible. Rules meant to guarantee consistency and connection-wide compliance limit local creativity and the capacity to organize according to context.

Most people who accept conference leadership responsibilities feel like Gulliver, waking up to discover that he couldn't move, being held back by thousands of little threads that restrict and confine, so numerous and intertwined that no single action cuts through to set you free.

Even though they operate with immense resources and much goodwill, the trajectory of most conferences predicts precipitous decline and eventual unsustainability. We risk failing in the fundamental task of making disciples of Jesus Christ for the transformation of the world.

It's time to think afresh about how conferences operate and to open ourselves to reinventing this fundamental unit of United Methodism.

Conversation Questions

What are your earliest memories and experiences of conference? Who were the people that defined for you what conference means? How did conference impact you, and what caused you to get involved?

How have you seen God at work through conference ministries? What are one or two signature ministries of your conference that operate with extraordinary effectiveness and fruitfulness?

When was a time when a conference program shaped your ministry, or strengthened the ministry of your church?

"Much conference work is unfocused, disconnected, unfruitful, perfunctory, or redundant." To what extent do you agree? When was a time you felt exasperated by conference committees or operations? What was the source of the frustration?

What would you estimate is the median age of those who participate in conference leadership, and how does this compare to the communities you serve? What does this mean?

How would you describe the relationship between your congregation and your conference? How would you gauge your own sense of belonging? Do you feel personally connected? Do you participate because you have to or because you want to?

When was a time that you underestimated the complexity of conference operations and the difficulty of leading change in a system with diffuse authority? When was a time that enough systems aligned to result in bold and fruitful ministry?

To what extent do you agree that the operational systems of conference are no longer conducive to our mission? What evidence would you offer that the system works, or that it doesn't function well?

Why Working Harder Isn't Helping

A well-known adage attributed to Edwards Deming says, "Systems are perfectly designed to get the results they are getting." If you and I were to stay up all night to devise a plan for associating churches, combining finances, and preparing and deploying leadership that would result in declining numbers, aging churches, unsustainable financial models, difficulty in recruiting young clergy, resistance to adaptation, and questionable relevance to next generations, we would design a system exactly like the one we have.

Before we explore the Seven Levers, we need to rethink some basic assumptions that underlie current operations in most conferences. Simply working harder, replacing people, or spending more money won't help until we identify systems that limit and restrain. The following four ideas shed light on assumptions that keep us stuck in systems that are no longer conducive to our mission.

The World Is Flat

Thomas Friedman's book, *The World Is Flat*, describes how globalization has become person-to-person.[1] People contact other people directly, personally, and immediately through mobile phones, the Internet, and Facebook. Instant communication, accessible technology, and reliable transportation have "flattened" the world so that persons form relationships and small businesses establish partnerships directly without large corporate or government channels. This has changed the world for journalists, retailers, music producers, banks, and universities. Anyone can access just about anything anytime from anywhere.

The same changes shape The United Methodist Church. Imagine a US congregation thirty years ago that felt called to supply clergy housing for United Methodist pastors in an African country. Before the Internet, the congregation depended upon conference staff to identify the means to make this happen. Because this involves work overseas, the idea was bumped up the hierarchy to a conference missions committee. If that committee agreed, they requested funding from the conference budget through the finance council. The annual conference would vote to support the work through apportionments or a special offering. Hundreds of churches would give money for parsonages in Africa through apportionments, many without knowing what they were supporting. The conference forwarded the accumulated funds up to the General Board of Global Ministries (GBGM). GBGM then transferred the funds down the other side of the pyramid to their administrative officer for Africa, who forwarded the funds to the bishop of the country targeted for mission, who distributed the money through superintendents to reach the congregations that need parsonages.

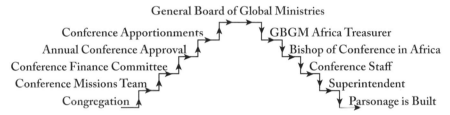

General Board of Global Ministries

Conference Apportionments   GBGM Africa Treasurer
Annual Conference Approval   Bishop of Conference in Africa
Conference Finance Committee   Conference Staff
Conference Missions Team   Superintendent
Congregation   Parsonage is Built

Up and over. Multiple steps. Centralized control. Complex systems. Slow processes.

Now imagine the same scenario today: a congregation feels called to build parsonages in Africa, a layperson surfs the Internet to explore options and evaluate existing channels, and then he or she directly contacts a pastor or superintendent in Africa. Connections are made, and the church transfers funds directly or assembles a Volunteers in Mission team to send to Africa to build parsonages.

Globalization is no longer conference to conference through general boards; it is person to person and church to church across the world.

Church  Church

Direct. Personal. Immediate. No up and over. The world is flat.

This flattened communication has huge implications. For instance, the Missouri Conference enjoys a longstanding partnership called the Mozambique Initiative. The project involves hundreds of church-to-church partnerships, pastor-to-pastor friendships, water well projects, salary supports, mutual prayers, and educational and medical ministries. Congregations send video greetings captured on cell phones for their partner churches to show during worship, and the partner church reciprocates. Visiting pastors or lay leaders greet hosts with genuine affection, inquiring about children and spouses they've never actually met but whom they've come to know through video calls and texting. Financial and in-kind gifts total millions of dollars, and the partnership involves minimal staff in Missouri and in Mozambique. The Mozambique Initiative reflects a new connectionalism sustained by direct personal relationships, congregational contact, and frequent communication with little superstructure or centralization.

More noteworthy, many churches do extensive global work with no conference involvement at all. One congregation raised more than $600,000 for work in Ghana, and sends work teams for construction, educational, and medical ministries. Smaller churches now support this work, which has no conference involvement at all.

These examples that contrast the old "up and over" approach with the flat new world seem self-evident. Less obvious are the many conference systems designed to go "up and over" in a flat world.

Conferences support campus ministries in an "up and over" fashion. A congregation three blocks from a university wants to offer a college-age ministry. We require that congregation to join with all other congregations to send apportionments to the conference where the higher education committee determines how much money to distribute to that particular campus. Personnel decisions, evaluations, and supervision rest with conference committees. The money goes up and comes back down three blocks away. The system fosters disinterest and an absence of personal engagement between the congregation and nearby campus.

"Up and over" is how United Methodists traditionally approach new church development. In many conferences, pastors or congregations who take initiative more directly are restrained. Our systems fight the new flat world.

In a flat world, churches start churches in their neighborhood, and even in other communities and other conferences. Congregations initiate student ministries at the campus down the street as well as at the university across the state where a number of their students attend.

Another implication of the flat world is that the "small can act large." Individuals can establish large platforms for influencing change, and congregations[2] have a greater impact than anyone ever imagined.

A single blogger can build an online community of hundreds of people. And congregations offer teaching events, sometimes with higher quality, greater participation, and more impact than conferences. The Church of the Resurrection's annual Leadership Institute includes quality workshops for churches of all sizes taught by a diversity of presenters and practitioners. Thousands of pastors, staff, and laypersons attend. Forty years ago, only seminaries or annual conferences provided such resources. Churches multiply their ministry in a flat world.

The flat world also changes the definition of collaboration. Collaboration previously meant keeping communication going with the people down the hall in the same department. Now collaboration means working together with anybody and everybody, even with competitors. My Dell laptop includes hardware and software from dozens of computer companies—Microsoft, IBM, Apple, Hewlett-Packard, Intel, Cisco Systems, and others. Competitors must collaborate in order for any of them to succeed.

In the flat world, conferences collaborate with local churches to start new congregations, conferences work with other conferences to initiate campus ministries, and conferences collaborate with foundations and universities for leadership training.

Conference leaders who give their best in systems that don't acknowledge the flat world find their work increasingly difficult and less relevant. Maintaining and enforcing "up and over" systems takes extraordinary energy in a flat world, and working harder to keep them going reaps fewer and fewer benefits. We struggle against this new world as something foreign, or we embrace it for the mission of the church.

The Giant Hairball

A second idea that explains why working harder isn't helping comes from Gordon McKenzie's delightful little book entitled *Orbiting the Giant Hairball*.[2] The *hairball* is MacKenzie's term for the procedures and policies that accumulate in an organization. Rules, standards, guidelines, and accepted models become established and set in stone. The "hairs" of the hairball begin as practices that initially solve a problem. Because the idea works in one place, it becomes prescribed in all places. Rules accumulate far beyond their usefulness. Every new policy adds another hair to the hairball. The hairball grows enormous, until it has its own heavy mass and gravity that pulls everything into the tangled web of established policies and procedures. The hairball makes change nearly impossible, stifles innovation, slows adaptive response, and chokes the spirit.

Have you experienced the intransigence of an organization that is stuck in place by its own collection of rules and procedures?

At last count, there were 4,774 shalls in the United Methodist *Book of Discipline* and hundreds more in conference standing rules, with paragraphs that begin, "The annual conference shall," "The congregation shall," and "The pastor shall." The *Discipline*'s description of a single conference board, Higher Education and Campus Ministry, extends into over sixty paragraphs, with nine pages about its composition, purpose, and tasks! Such detailed prescriptions limit the work of conferences. Obviously, we need standard order for the essentials, but we don't improve and expand the mission of the church each time we mandate a requirement. There are dozens of reasons why any new idea can't be done. Many conference meetings merely feed the insatiable beast with more resolutions and amendments that perpetuate a self-reinforcing system.

Orbiting is MacKenzie's phrase for responsible creative imagination, vigorously exploring options, and remaining close enough to the organization to benefit from the physical, intellectual, and relational resources without becoming entombed in the bureaucracy. *Orbiting* suggests a healthier way for pastors and congregations to relate to the conference, and for creative conferences to relate to the general church.

Hairball is policy, procedure, imperative, rigidity, submission, and regimented similarity, while *orbiting* is originality, nonconformity, initiative, experimentation, flexibility, risk, and adaptation.[3]

Our propensity to solve everything by creating rules that must apply to everyone else creates an operational nightmare. Conference organizational charts, nominations processes, and budgeting requirements are prescribed in extraordinary detail and in ways that serve a thousand secondary purposes rather than the mission. They make effectiveness and alignment almost impossible. Exasperated leaders constantly try to work around unhelpful requirements.

If you had a great idea, where would you take it, and how would it be received, perfected, approved, funded, and executed? How does a creative idea move through your conference from initial spark to fruitful ministry?

Most conference systems include five to seven layers of organizational approval. Each person or committee has the ability to say *No*, but nobody has the authority to say *Yes*.[4]

Younger generations have zero tolerance for the hairball (except for those we've trained to think this is the way United Methodism works!). In the world young people live in, many things happen at once with extraordinary immediacy. They expect quick responses and rapid action.

Our endless entanglement of rules makes us seem irrelevant to the world around us. Our focus on internal mechanisms draws our attention back in upon ourselves and away from the mission field. The hairball turns away the next generations of leaders. Complexity is the silent killer of organizations.

Nonprofits Are Different

Jim Collins's *Good to Great and the Social Sector*[5] provides insights into why nonprofit organizations are difficult to lead and how ordinary business models don't apply. Change through formal structures becomes nearly impossible with leadership diffusely distributed across various people, boards, and committees.

Most people picture a pyramid structure with the bishop on top. In fact, in United Methodist conferences, no one is on top of anything! Bishops hold authority over cabinets and their personal staff. Council directors work with leadership teams nominated and elected by the annual conference. The laity elects lay leaders. Boards of Ordained Ministry operate independently from cabinets. The treasurer works for the Council of Finance and Administration. Retreat ministries and districts own their own property with their own personnel and policies.

Conferences have no concentrated executive power. As a result, bishops, council chairs, lay leaders, and conference staff appear less decisive, less focused, and more reserved in exercising authority than business leaders in similar-sized corporations. Jim Collins writes that they "only appear that way to those who fail to grasp the complex governance and diffuse power structures common to social sectors."[6] In the business world, the executive leader has enough concentrated power to make decisions. In diffuse nonprofit organizations, no one—including the nominal chief executive—has enough structural power to make things happen.

This is not to suggest that we should embed more structural authority in bishops, board chairs, or anyone else. Rather, we should realize that leadership in conferences relies less on hierarchical power and more on persuasion, appealing to mutual values, the power of common language, and the influence of coalition.

For instance, one of the most important tools any leader has is the ability to influence personnel decisions. In United Methodist conferences, authority doesn't rest with bishops but is distributed throughout the conference system, with District Committees on Ministries, superintendents, senior pastors, pastor-parish relations committees, and the Board of Ordained Ministry all playing significant roles for clergy; and the finance committee, personnel committee, and camping board fulfilling similar responsibilities for staff.

And to whom is the bishop accountable? The conference committee on episcopacy? The jurisdictional committee on episcopacy? The College of Bishops?

Each of these supervising bodies may be driven by differing values. A results-oriented focus on fruitfulness may be resisted, or each entity may have its own outcomes that conflict with larger conference priorities. In business, desired results are more clearly identified: enough customers, revenue, clients, the bottom line. In nonprofit organizations, it's more difficult to assess performance related to the mission, especially if that mission is unclear or ill defined.

In such a diffuse organization, everyone believes that things should change, but they can't agree on what matters most, what each is expected to do, or how to measure progress. Leaders can't select the people they need, they have difficultly removing people who are ineffective, and it's nearly impossible to stop doing things that aren't working, even when everyone knows they're not working.

A system with such diffusely distributed authority requires leadership by consensus on a limited number of critical issues and by appealing to common values. Mandates don't work, and plans that dictate compliance from all boards, pastors, or churches are ineffective.

In the absence of concentrated executive authority, many conferences rely on legislative authority to develop focus. They turn to annual conference sessions for direction and change. The *Discipline* embeds innumerable tasks in the annual conference itself as a collective body.

Developing strategies becomes nearly impossible with huge numbers of people who bring widely divergent agendas. Large venues are impossible for focused, deliberate change.

Working harder using only executive authority and legislation will continue to exasperate leaders. We need other tools to lead.

The goal, according to Collins, is not to make nonprofits more businesslike, because most businesses also operate in mediocre fashions, even with executive authority.[7] The goal is to operate toward the mission with excellence and fruitfulness.

Fading Relevance

And simply working harder isn't helping because our way of doing things appears less relevant and more distant from real world needs than ever before. Approaching our complex and outdated systems is like stepping into a time machine that takes us back to another age of complex bureaucracies, convoluted systems, obscure rules, quaint traditions, endless reports, and infinitely slow processes.

The Towers-Watson Report finds that people outside the church perceive most of what we do as irrelevant to their lives and to the needs of the world. This crisis of relevance is especially true for next generations. How do our conferences, with all their millions of dollars, dozens of staff, hundreds of volunteers, and zillions of meetings have any demonstrable bearing on the mission of Christ? So much of the activity seems pointless, or at least extraneous, to the real-life needs and suffering in the world around us or to the vitality and capacity of congregations to address those needs.

The risk of irrelevance has several dimensions. First, as David Kinnaman and Gabe Lyons have described in *UnChristian*, younger generations view Christians in general as judgmental, antihomosexual, hypocritical, old-fashioned, too political, out of touch with reality, insensitive to others, and boring.[8] Most people around us, and especially young people, perceive our endless debates, reliance on meetings, and internal squabbles as unattractive and as impediments to serving. They view our way of doing things as unapproachable, impenetrable, confusing, ineffective, and irrelevant.

A second form of fading relevance is described in the Towers-Watson Report as the growing distance between the people in the pew and the leaders of the denomination, including those who serve at the conference level. The things that matter most to the everyday Christian seeking to grow in grace and searching for channels to serve are not the same things that fill the agendas of conference meetings. Detailed descriptions about how apportionments are used by conferences, general boards, or the Council of Bishops leave people blurry eyed rather than highly motivated.

Another risk of irrelevance is found in how large churches, or growing churches of any size, view their relationship to their conferences. Pastors view conferences as restraining influences that draw resources away from vital ministry, restrict personnel development, limit mission initiative by requiring participation in particular programs, and squelch plans for congregationally launched new churches. Laity perceive conferences issues as remote and unrelated to the work of the congregations. Conferences desire a closer relationship to their congregations than congregations want with their conferences.

And younger clergy question the relevance of conference itself. As one described to me,

> None of what happens seems relevant to my ministry. All the meetings and committees and budgets seem like spinning wheels. Everything is focused on the medium instead of the mission, on keeping the internal mechanisms going. I'm not sure how it relates to the mission of Christ. Volunteering to serve on a committee is like being sucked into a black hole. Suddenly you're going to all kinds of meetings that really don't matter.

"Up and over" systems in a flat world, the hairball of rules and procedures, impractical executive authority and ineffective legislative solutions, and the perception that our work is irrelevant—is it any wonder that working harder isn't helping?

Conversation Questions

Describe some examples from your own conference of already doing ministry person-to-person and church-to-church in a flat world instead of "up and over." What long-term implications do you see for conference operations?

What "up and over" systems does your conference use that could be done differently in a flat world?

How does MacKenzie's notion of an organizational hairball help you understand some of your experiences in church leadership? Can you identify times when you or a committee got tangled in policy and rules that limited or distracted from ministry?

When was a time you successfully navigated organizational restraints to offer fresh and innovative ministry? What were the obstacles? How did you do it?

How do we avoid unknowingly contributing to organizational intransigence? As a leader, how do you help sustain the life of the Spirit and of community in Christ as something fluid, alive, and flowing rather than as something stuck and static?

What "hairball" policies and procedures limit creative response in your conference? In your congregation?

Leaders in a nonprofit organization without concentrated executive power often appear less decisive, less focused, and more reserved than leaders of similar-sized businesses. Have you seen examples of that in your conference? In your congregation? Are there benefits to diffuse structures?

When was a time that something couldn't get done because no one had the authority to act? How does a diffuse organization make it nearly impossible to stop doing things that don't work?

Kinnaman and Lyons say younger generations view Christians in general as judgmental, antihomosexual, hypocritical, old-fashioned, too political, out of touch with reality, insensitive to others, and boring. How does that ring true in your experience? What does this mean for congregations? For the conference? How do you suppose your conference operations, committees, and work are perceived by younger generations?

FINDING FOCUS

Disciplined planning, disciplined people, disciplined governance, and disciplined allocation of resources—these are the keys, according to Jim Collins, for effectiveness in nonprofits as well as businesses.[1]

Conference leaders may be tempted to jump immediately to the Seven Levers in an attempt to adopt them and integrate them into their conference operations. But it becomes impossible to agree on the fundamental strategies to move forward without first finding some basic level of clarity and consensus about why a conference exists, what values drive our behavior, and what a conference is meant to accomplish. Focusing comes first.

Several conferences are finding focus and exploring ways to align their resources for the mission of the church. No one enjoys perfect success, but everyone learns from these experiments.

This chapter outlines one attempt by a conference to give sustained attention to a focused mission with common expectations and clear priorities. No one suggests that the Missouri Conference has everything figured out, and we never say, "You ought to do it this way." We invite anyone interested to step into our workshop and to look over our shoulders to see how we do things on an operational basis. We share what we've learned, talk about what works, and offer caution about what doesn't. The purpose is to provoke reflection and conversation about your own conference. This is an invitation to join a conversation. Our approaches are open to debate, and other conferences will come to other conclusions about methods and priorities.

The Context

The Missouri Conference in 2004 comprised nearly nine hundred congregations, 176,000 United Methodists, with an average worship attendance of eighty-four thousand people. Like most conferences, the Missouri area had declined by nearly eighty thousand members during the previous forty years, with attendance decreasing every year during that time.

Several variables made Missouri distinct. Missouri had recently merged two predecessor conferences, disrupting traditional roles, relationships, and governance structures. As in the children's game of musical chairs, the music was still playing in 2004 and people had not yet grabbed on tightly to their new positions. There was more fluidity and less rigidity than in most conferences. Also in that year, Missouri received a new bishop, and in early 2005 a lawsuit that had been winding through the courts for several years culminated in a financial judgment against the conference that exceeded total financial assets, creating a greater sense of urgency than losing eighty thousand people ever had.

Missouri had several strengths—talented and committed lay and clergy leadership, a signature missions ministry, a partnership with Mozambique, and a twenty-five year history of starting new congregations with notable success. Like most conferences, Missouri struggled with increasing conference and general church expenses, decreasing membership, increasing average ages, and the challenge of mobilizing such an incredibly complex organization in a way that maximized impact.

Initially, I had difficulty locating an appropriate governing body with which to do strategic planning. More than fifty people served on the conference council, which was organized according to the *Book of Discipline*. Dedicated leaders were eager to help, but the size and composition of the council made it principally a reporting body rather than one suited for disciplined conversation. Identifying priorities was difficult because of the representative nature of the council, which fostered an understandable tendency for members to protect and promote the particular geographic area or ministry or board represented. Members felt frustrated, meetings ran long, and attendance was low. The council felt unwieldy, and unrelated to the cabinet, Council on Finance and Administration (CFA), or other entities. As bishop, I felt like a guest anytime I visited—greeted warmly, invited to share a few words, and then sitting passively through reports. Mission statements were so generalized as to be unhelpful in aligning resources or motivating action. "Growing, learning, leading, and serving" were the words used to set priorities, but these were not specific enough to suggest what people should work on.

To get a better handle on how the conference was perceived, I collaborated with the lay leader and council director to lead a series of conversations across the conference, inviting twenty pastors and laity to each gathering. We encouraged honest and in-depth conversation about the work of conference. These were not gripe sessions but attempts to explore appropriate roles for conference, priorities, and opportunities. We took notes and learned much. Following these sessions, we formed Pathways, which for the next eighteen months became the principal work team and think tank for reconceptualizing the conference.

The Authority to Convene

In a system with no executive authority, diffuse leadership structures, and complex legislative layering, conference leaders turn to alternative tools to identify priorities and influence direction. An underutilized tool is *the authority to convene*. While bishops, lay leaders, and conference staff may have limited formal authority, any one of these at any time can invite together anybody they wish for conversation, exploration, and learning.

Pathways represents such a gathering. Pathways had no formal authority derived from the *Discipline* or conference rules.

Pathways explored the purpose, role, and mission of our conference. What are the essential tasks that must be done with excellence? What does it mean to be a conference in the twenty-first century, and how does this derive from our Wesleyan roots? What does conference do well, and where can it improve? What does it do that doesn't need to be done or that can be done better by someone else? We primarily focused on conference operations—what we do, how we do it, and why it matters for the mission of Christ. We imagined a different future. The conversations were invigorating, honest, intense, and extraordinarily helpful.

We wanted creative, gifted people to join Pathways based on their ability to lead fruitful ministry and for their openness to new ideas and their knowledge and experience with organizations. We wanted change agents, including laity and pastors of all sizes of churches. We wanted people who would participate because they "get to" rather than because they "have to." Pathways was diverse in age, gender, theology, clergy status, church size, and ethnicity. We searched for people who wouldn't inordinately defend or justify any existing program or staff position. Most participants served on a conference team, but none were selected to represent constituencies. Only three were invited based on their formal office—the lay leader, the chair of finance, and the chair of the Board of Ordained Ministry. One conference staff member and one superintendent participated. Others were people capable of playing well with others, passionately in love with Christ and The United Methodist Church, and yet unafraid to offer critical reflection. These were people willing to invest in change.

The name *Pathways* was purposeful. We avoided terms such as *restructuring, task force, subcommittee,* or other language that connoted merely structural change or that elicited an immediate "here we go again" response. After all, every conference in United Methodism has restructured numerous times in recent years. We avoided terms like *long-term planning,* which connotes linear organizational processes, or *futures,* which once was trendy but now feels retro. *Pathways* looks forward, implies movement, and suggests a direction rather than preconceived outcomes. It resonates with notions of spiritual journey, exploration, and stepping forward in faith. We used the plural because there are many paths forward.

I explain this not to recommend the name to others but to suggest care in choosing names for such work. What does the title communicate? Another round of reshuffling conference committees? Or something more hopeful, less linear, more creative, fresher and more inviting? People want to know, "Will something finally change?" Cynicism about past initiatives presents considerable obstacles in recruiting potential leaders and developing trust with pastors and laity.

The Authority to Select Leadership

The formation of a leadership team is critical, and involves several significant but highly nuanced decisions.

An early decision relates to who selects the team and on what basis. In most instances, planning teams are elected by either the annual conference itself or by the conference council. This can create immediate limitations on the ability to lead significant change.

Hierarchies are inherently risk averse and resistant to change, and the more complex and diffuse an organization, the more its individual components crave stability and cling to their habits. When we ask the annual conference, through its nominating process, or the conference council to identify leadership for a committee meant to lead change, we almost guarantee that the resulting team will replicate the same limitations as the body that elects them.

John Kotter, in a *Harvard Business Review* article, describes the dynamics of selecting leadership from *within* existing hierarchies.[2] This works well for simple linear tasks that move an organization from point A to a well-defined point B (forming a task force to prepare a job description, for instance), but this doesn't work well for initiating significant directional change. Instead, the key is selecting a few people from within the hierarchy and a larger number of people from throughout the network who are invested in change, driven by a sense of urgency, and have the expertise needed by the team. For United Methodists, the larger network, which provides a rich pool to select from, is the connection, the clergy and laity throughout the annual conference. This decreases the risk of simply confirming existing systems or replicating the culture. Conference systems need fresh eyes and new ideas rather than business as usual.

If the first tool available to leaders in a diffuse organization is the authority to convene, the second is *the authority to identify and select leadership.* The selection of twenty people for Pathways, in consultation with the lay leader and council director, violated no paragraphs of the *Discipline* or standing rules. Operating outside of established structures did create tension between the newly formed Pathways and the existing leadership teams. It unavoidably stimulated suspicion and made formally elected leaders and conference staff feel left out.

Pathways had no formal authority. Its formation created a parallel leadership system, and its parallel nature provided checks and balances. Pathways leaders knew that any innovation would have to eventually be voted upon by the conference council, CFA, the trustees, and the annual conference. Pathways was free to imagine and create but had to prepare recommendations that were reasonable and compelling enough for the formal hierarchy to accept. The changes proposed by Pathways couldn't have been generated through the existing structures even though those same systems eventually approved the recommendations.

In *Leading Change*, John Kotter describes the significance of a guiding coalition.[3] Major change can't happen because of a single leader, bishop, lay leader, board chair, or staff member. To have a chance at real change, the guiding coalition must have significant credibility based on the experience and expertise of the members. It must have enough key players from significant components of the organization to have sufficient influence. And it must have people with proven *leadership* skills and not merely *management* abilities.

To develop a vision and strategies helpful to the mission (and acceptable to those who will eventually approve them) requires mutual trust, and this takes considerable conversation. Pathways worked together for eighteen months, discussing, researching, and planning, before we presented proposals for conference approval. Creativity doesn't operate on the principles of efficiency, and we needed time for ideas to ripen, for hope to build, for exploration and research. We encountered many frustrations, dead ends, contradictions, and moments of hopelessness and conflict. We also discovered times of clarity, insight, unity, and consensus.

The Authority To Set the Agenda

A third tool available for leaders in a complex organization with diffusely distributed power is *the authority to set the agenda*. Ronald Heifetz has said that attention is the currency of leadership.[4] People expect leaders to select the issues that warrant attention. Rather than accepting a variety of agendas composed of the hundreds of concerns emanating from existing boards and ministries, Pathways was able to say, "We have one main focus—the mission and purpose of annual conference." We could dig deep, and then dig even deeper. We read literature on organizations, leadership, and mission to focus our conversations. We drew the attention of Pathways toward what was most fundamental for our future without the dizzying distractions of trying to solve multitudes of issues presented by the dozens of moving parts. We distilled to the essentials.

Another critical decision for forming a guiding coalition is determining who leads the process. I led Pathways, not because I was the bishop but because this work matches my gifts. Other conferences have involved outside consultants, or they've invited a layperson or clergyperson who has experience in such work. This works if the process leader brings excellent credentials to the task and isn't perceived as representing a particular constituency that would inordinately influence outcomes. No matter who leads, the bishop's visible presence, support, and involvement is nevertheless critical. I once served on a restructuring task force and wrote the final recommendations. The bishop didn't participate, and his absence was felt at every meeting. We never knew whether we had the leadership capital to see the process through.

The formation of a team such as Pathways likely sounds familiar to most readers. Many conferences have gone through similar processes, some of them multiple times. Rethinking purpose and practice is hard work, and we can't outsource our vision to a consultant or simply borrow another conference's plan and expect it to work for us. However, people view the forming of a team with cynicism, perceiving that this merely "rearranges the deckchairs on the Titanic" and won't result in change. Enthusiasm falls if operations return to the status quo. To avoid this requires doing everything possible to reduce the risks of unfocused work, ill-defined outcomes, blurry mission statements, and results that give no real direction to the work of the conference.

Pathways ultimately recommended a straightforward mission statement for the conference, noted five common expectations and five congregational practices, and identified two critical priorities.

Nothing sounds particularly original, but the work to arrive at these reshaped the leadership of the conference. As we crafted and recrafted the mission statement, narrowed the expectations from fifteen to eight to five by sharpening definitions, and isolated priorities from four, to three, and finally to two, the conversations reshaped our conference and our understanding of our various roles. We were changed.

Pathways offered directional orientation and clarity of mission with only a few basic structural changes. The entire recommendation fit on one page. If the conference council, CFA, lay leader, and annual conference accepted the recommendations, the details would be refined by the committees for their respective responsibilities. Pathways would exist for a few months in the interim.

Pathways requested a called session of annual conference for two hours to either adopt or reject the one-page outline. During the six weeks leading up to the called session, I and others involved in Pathways led conversations across the conference to teach, listen, and respond to questions.

The plan's adoption at the called session in March empowered other committees and staff to begin work immediately on changes to standing rules, budgets, and job descriptions in time for approval at our scheduled June conference.

Nothing was borrowed wholesale from others, nothing was entirely original, nothing was top down, nothing was rushed, and nothing was accidental. And yet because of Pathways, nothing remained entirely the same.

The Power of a Common Language

On the wall in each room in our conference center is a poster that reads:

The Missouri Conference—

Leading Congregations to Lead People to
Actively Follow Jesus Christ

Five Expectations:

Christ-Centered, Fruitfulness, Excellence,
Accountability, Collaboration

Five Practices:

Radical Hospitality, Passionate Worship,
Intentional Faith Development,
Risk-Taking Mission and Service, Extravagant Generosity.

That's it. No more. No less. The words are the fruit of the Pathways conversations. After they were adopted at the called session of annual conference in March 2006, they have directed the work of the conference. I've probably described their meaning in conversation, presentation, preaching, and teaching more than five hundred times, and so have our lay leaders, pastors, team chairs, conference staff, and superintendents. Teams revisit those words in nearly every meeting.

In a large complex organization with diffusely distributed authority, a fourth underutilized tool available to leaders is *the power of a common language*. Words that give direction to behavior, value, and attitude do more to align, motivate, and unite than any restructuring chart or newly adopted policies. They may change a few things by one hundred percent, or they may change a hundred things by one percent—either way, their power and influence are remarkable.

Pathways spent considerable time seeking the best ways to articulate the unique mission of the annual conference. The mission of The United Methodist Church is to make disciples of Jesus Christ for the transformation of the world. Congregations play a role in that mission, as do pastors and laity and chaplains and institutions and general boards.

But what is the particular role that conferences play in the mission of The United Methodist Church?

Conferences don't make disciples. They don't baptize babies, counsel newlyweds, conduct funerals, or form recovery ministries. Conferences don't teach Bible studies or provide pastoral care or solicit volunteers for soup kitchens. Congregations do these things. The *Discipline* appropriately describes congregations as "the most significant arena through which disciple-making occurs."[5]

Conferences aren't on the front lines. They aren't where the action is when it comes to the mission of the church. Conferences are a step or two removed from making disciples. By analogy, soldiers and equipment operate on the front lines where lives are at stake every day. But the soldiers in the field require support from behind, where complex systems provide food, fuel, recruitment, training, medical support, and strategy. Even highly localized commands require coordinated support systems.

In a similar way, conferences help the helpers and serve the servers. *Leading Congregations to Lead People to Actively Follow Christ* seems simple and self-evident. And yet this statement fundamentally turns preexisting perceptions upside down. Implied is the notion that congregations do not exist to support the conference but that conferences exist to serve, strengthen, and multiply congregations.

John Wesley didn't create churches, chapels, and faith communities so that one day he would have a conference to preside over. He created conference to unite, energize, strengthen, and empower faith communities and to resource them with leadership.

Pathways avoided wishy-washy, generalized, or blurry statements that provide no clues to what leaders are supposed to do. The mission statement is concise enough to direct work, shape conversation, and give priority, while being widely applicable so as to be helpful in hundreds of different settings. And it is brief. Conferences often mistakenly act as if *more* is *more*, creating long lists of values and objectives. *Less* is *more* when it comes to a common language.

Imagine every conversation undergoing a measure of scrutiny relative to this mission statement. When trustees or CFA discuss insurance, they wrestle with questions like, "How does this impact the congregation's capacity to do ministry?" In cabinet, what if someone asked, "Does our decision help or harm congregations?" Imagine the treasurer working on tool kits for congregations that want help or the mission director training churches for disaster relief.

The mission statement directs the flow of energy and attention. It causes us to redouble our effort on some tasks while abandoning other tasks altogether. And it causes us to constantly ask, "Is this decision for the convenience of the conference or the good of congregations? Does this action restrain congregations or set them free? Does this increase fruitful ministry or make congregations more dependent?"

If a mission statement doesn't prompt an organization to engage some work it hasn't done before as well as cause the organization to stop some things it has previously done, then it fails to offer direction. Mission statements say that we are going to go *that* way instead of *this* way. They operate as a compass. We may not always move true north, but with a compass we know which way we're going and can correct course as necessary.

In addition to the mission statement, the conference adopted five expectations that also provide direction and are second only to the mission statement in their importance. Pathways deliberated over what these words represent. Are these *values*? *Qualities*? *Hopes*? A *common rule of practice*?

Values was too nebulous, ethereal, and passive for us. *Rules* or *standards* connoted more rigidity than we intended and sounded patronizing. We agreed to call these *expectations*.

These are what we expect of each other. It's fair for churches to expect these of the conference and for the conference to expect these of churches, for laity to expect these of clergy and vice versa. It's fair to expect these of supervisors and bishops and committees and youth leaders and events and meetings and in all our work together.

First, we expect of each other that our work is *Christ-centered*, that our ministry derives from Christ, leads to Christ, and is done in the spirit of Christ. The conference, and the churches that comprise it, do not belong to the trustees, the bishop, the pastors, or the laity but to Christ alone. The church has no mission apart from the mission of God in Jesus Christ, and so we saturate our work with prayer, with a searching for Christ through scripture, openness to Christ through worship, and by seeking the face of Christ in those we serve. This expectation drives how we treat each other, how we minister with the poor, how we form community, and how we understand our witness in the world.

Second, we expect *fruitfulness* of each other and our ministries. Scripture is replete with references to seeds, sowers, soils, trees, vines, branches, farmers, vineyards, and harvests. These draw our attention to the result, impact, and outcome of ministry as seen in changed lives and a transformed world. Jesus said, "If you remain in me and I in you, then you will produce much fruit. . . . My Father is glorified when you produce much fruit and in this way prove that you are my disciples" (John 15:5, 8). We don't congratulate ourselves on inputs (such as the size of budgets, the numbers of staff, the quality of facilities) but by the actual impact and fruit of our work. We measure, experiment, learn, and evaluate. We feed ministries that bear fruit, and we stop doing things that don't. It's fair for the conference to expect fruitfulness from pastors and for churches to expect fruitfulness from conference ministries. We expect fruitfulness in campus ministries, youth work, and seminaries as well as from water-well projects and medical missions that we support across the globe.

Third, we expect *excellence* from each other. By excellence, Pathways doesn't refer to business models that ratchet up competitive or disruptive instincts but to the language of excellence used in scripture: "I'm going to show you an even better way" (1 Cor 12:31), and "Be the best in this work of grace in the same way that you are the best in everything" (2 Cor 8:7). Are we offering our best with every ministry? Every workshop, training event, seminar, camping experience, youth ministry, or session of conference—is it characterized by superb planning, content, and leadership? We should expect nothing less.

Fourth, we expect *accountability* from each other. Jesus sent the disciples out "in pairs" (Luke 10:1), because in community, we discover accountability. Imagine two disciples walking on the road to a place they'd never been before with a message that was new to them to preach before a crowd that was likely hostile. By sending disciples in pairs, Jesus intended for them to talk each other into greater boldness, pray for each other, and support each other. And when the disciples returned to the road after teaching, what do you suppose they talked about? "I can't believe you said that!" or "You did great!" That's accountability.

It's fair to expect accountability throughout the system—transparency regarding finances, responsible use of resources, integrity in leadership, and evaluation for clergy, staff, superintendents, and the bishop.

Fifth, we expect *collaboration*. Everyone owns the outcomes, and so we help one another out across departments, boards, and districts. We learn and borrow from everyone, and we share everything we can. Staff members work in their distinct fields, but the fields have swinging gates that allow easy passage into adjacent areas to seek or offer help.

These five expectations seem so simple that they hardly deserve attention, and yet they drive conversations related to appointments, resource allocation, evaluation, and programming on a daily basis.

Pathways could have listed a dozen more expectations, and some people want to add prayer, diversity, young people, honesty, service, leading, or other worthy words. We felt like these five communicated the essentials.

In addition to the mission statement and five expectations, Pathways also named the five practices to provide a template for congregational work. Because I wrote *Five Practices of Fruitful Congregations*, people are sometimes surprised that the conference doesn't put nearly as much focus on the five practices in daily operations as we do on the five expectations. The five practices are about healthy congregations while the expectations are about our life and work together as a conference.

The wide use of a common language reflected in our mission state-ment, expectations, and practices has been instrumental in helping the conference identify common strategies. We continue to redefine these terms, and their meaning deepens with each new ministry and with the passage of time. The common language has fostered consensus across the diffuse and complex network of ministries that comprise our conference, without relying on top-down mandates, executive authority, or convoluted legislative processes. They give enough guidance to provide direction with enough room for contextual decision making to foster creativity.

A common language allows leaders to step into any context, rehearse the mission and expectations, and then ask, "Tell me what you've been working on that moves this forward. What have you learned? And what do you plan to do next?" With a common language, diverse groups contribute to the mission on their own terms.

The Authority to Clarify Priorities

A fifth tool for leaders in a large complex system with diffusely distrib-uted power is *the authority to clarify priorities*.

What fundamental activities are so critical to the mission of the con-ference that failure to perform them with excellence will unquestionably lead to the decline of the organization? Pathways wrestled with this ques-tion for months. Conferences work on hundreds of different projects and balance dozens of priorities. Which are most important? Which activities comprise the core process because they are so critical that the conference cannot fulfill its mission—leading congregations to lead people to actively follow Christ—unless these are done consistently well?

Pathways whittled down the list to two essential tasks: congregational excellence and pastoral excellence. Identifying these priorities laid the foundation for strategies that became the most critical levers for change.

Congregational excellence includes how well the conference starts new congregations, supports growing congregations, intervenes in de-clining congregations, multiplies the work of large congregations, teaches congregational leadership, fosters congregational innovation, forms congregations for emerging populations, and closes congregations as they approach the end of their life cycle. Without vibrant, fruitful, growing congregations, there will be no conference, no missions, no social witness, no camps, and no pastors and laity in the future. Congregational health is non-negotiable for any vision of the future.

Pastoral excellence refers to how well a conference recruits, mentors, educates, trains, credentials, deploys, supervises, evaluates, and at times, removes, those who lead congregations. Fruitful, effective pastors are essential, and if our systems don't provide streams of excellent leadership, then congregations suffer, lose focus, decline, and die. The conference cannot succeed in its mission without effective leaders.

Identifying these two critical elements has monumental implications for organizing the work of the conference, lending focus to staff, structuring our governance, and guiding the use of time for the bishop, cabinet, and the boards and committees of the conference.

Based on these two elements of our core process—congregational excellence and pastoral excellence—Pathways recommended a more streamlined organizational plan, reworked the role of conference directors, and began to focus on these priorities.

A Focusing Organization

Leading a large complex organization with multiple points of authority doesn't require having every single entity in absolute alignment, perfectly focused on one or two goals. That will never happen in our conferences, and it's unrealistic to expect it.

Leading conferences requires identifying priorities clearly enough that all the components can join the work of focusing their attention and activity toward critical points of convergence. When enough of the various components do this—the bishop, the cabinet, lay leaders, the conference council, the staff—then momentum builds for serious change. An effective conference is a *focusing* organization rather than a perfectly *focused* one. The difference may seem subtle, but is really quite significant.

As a birder, I carry a pair of binoculars everywhere I travel. Learning to use the binoculars well requires knowing how to locate the bird I'm looking for and then adjusting the focus so I can see clearly enough to identify the most detailed markings. Inevitably, as soon as I focus, the bird shifts, flutters, or hops just enough to require me to refocus. My binoculars are never finally focused; rather, I'm continually focusing and refocusing with slight movements of my fingers in nearly imperceptible degrees.

Focusing implies continuous but incomplete action. Focusing never ends. Focusing is hard work. The mission field shifts, conditions within the conference change, and people step into and out of positions of leadership. Nothing remains static. The goal is to have a *focusing* organization rather than a *focused* one.

Once everyone knows what is most important to work on, experiments begin here and there, sometimes emerging from conference committees or more likely from congregations, pastors, and lay leaders. From these experiments, strategies take form that clarify direction even further. Clear strategies shape a conference the way passing a magnet over iron shavings causes them to align—not every individual piece readjusts, but enough do to form a discernible pattern.

With clearly defined strategies conferences operate with a sense of imperative. People discern forward motion. Everyone takes a next step. A common mission fosters changes in attitudes, values, and behaviors. The culture shifts, and focusing continues.

The Seven Levers did not spring forth overnight as well-defined strategies. They emerged slowly from experiments and experiences of conferences across the connection. As more conferences became better at focusing resources toward critical points for change, consensus emerged about what works best and how some strategies have enormous effect. These strategies, even when applied with distinctly different tactics, have disproportionate influence on the direction of conferences.

Strategies are the fruit of disciplined planning, thinking, work, and allocation of resources. Such focusing by a number of conferences has unleashed the creativity and experimentation that has led to the Seven Levers.

Conversation Questions

How does your conference do in-depth, disciplined strategic planning? Who takes responsibility for leading it? How do constituents participate?

When have you seen a leader exercise the authority to convene in order to address an unmet need by gathering together leaders outside of their formal roles? How did it work?

What are the risks of relying on existing committees, staff, and boards to lead change? What are the risks of working outside of existing committees and staff?

When has your conference formed an effective guiding coalition to address a significant challenge? How did it work? What limited its effectiveness? What would you suggest doing differently?

The conference described in this chapter narrowed its focus to a single mission statement, five expectations, and five practices. What's the benefit of focusing on so few elements? What's the drawback? When is a mission statement too limiting? And when is it too expansive? Why is it so hard to focus a conference?

How does your conference, or your congregation, use a common language to give direction to work? How well has the language taken hold?

How would you describe the mission of your annual conference? Would others describe it in a similar manner? How well does your conference's stated purpose shape priorities, align budgets, and direct work?

What are the activities that are so critical to your conference's mission that failure to perform them with excellence will lead to decline? How would you suggest aligning resources and staff accordingly?

The First Lever

A Strategy for Starting New Churches

Levers help us get things done. The advantage of using a lever is that we can move things that otherwise we could never budge, and heavy loads can be lifted with limited strength. Levers make impossible tasks doable.

In physics, a lever amplifies an input force to provide a greater output force. The English word *lever* derives from the French *levant*, which means *to raise*. Levers help us lift things that would ordinarily be too heavy to lift, defying the downward forces of gravity with less effort than would otherwise be necessary. Fifty pounds of effort can lift one hundred pounds of weight with a properly working lever.

Organizationally, levers are critical operational focal points for change that allow leaders to derive disproportionate results relative to the amount of work and resources invested. They are fundamental strategies that use our finite resources to greatest effect, making progress against the otherwise unmovable forces of intransigence and decline.

Levers multiply results. Each lever leads to multiple system-wide consequences. Levers aren't necessarily the easiest places to effect change, but successful work in these areas fosters sustainable long-term benefits. These seven levers rise to the top because of the extraordinary consensus of research and experience that has developed on the importance of these strategies.

New Congregations

The first lever is a strategy for starting new churches. Conferences intent on increasing the number of vital congregations develop an assertive, sustainable, fruitful plan for planting congregations. No conference plan for reversing decline can succeed without starting congregations.

Twenty-five percent of the worship attendance in the Missouri Conference is in congregations started during the last thirty-five years. Thirteen of the twenty-five congregations with the highest attendance were either new church starts or relocations during that period. Last Easter, 2,700 people attended worship in churches started during the past five years in the single district that serves downtown St. Louis. Nearly 18 percent of apportionments are given by churches started between 1978 and 2012. (These statistics don't include the eighteen thousand members of Church of the Resurrection, which was founded by the Missouri Conference but moved across the border that splits Kansas City.)

These numbers aren't unique to Missouri. Six of the twenty-five largest congregations in the North Georgia Conference are new church starts during recent decades, and attendance in new churches accounts for 14 percent of the conference's total attendance. Several conferences could report similar statistics.

With my assignment to Missouri, I inherited a rich tradition of starting new congregations. The conference was one of the leaders in the jurisdictions in successful starts. Continuing that legacy required persistence. Five US congregations planted in the last five years already have more than one thousand people, and two of those are in Missouri.

Why are new church plants important? The statistical evidence demonstrates convincingly that new congregations reach unchurched people more effectively than existing congregations. Demographically, new congregations do better at reaching younger generations and more diverse populations, which are the fastest growing segments of our communities. New churches find it easier to experiment with new models of ministry.[1]

This replicates the experience of congregations who seek to increase participation in discipling groups. Is it easier to achieve an increase of twenty young adults by pressuring a long-standing, middle-aged Sunday school class to assimilate them, or to initiate a new group focused on young adults using resources attuned to their needs? People exploring spirituality afresh connect more easily to people like themselves than they do to long-standing, tightly knit groups. New attracts new.

New congregations naturally focus outward. They have no "inward" to focus on yet—no buildings, infrastructure, cliquishness, traditions, or territories to defend—and their very existence depends upon their capacity to reach new people. They can't afford to waste money, and so they tightly contain costs, use highly motivated volunteers, and streamline governance. Every person has a discipleship task in the early life of a congregation. They focus on the mission field, highly attuned to their neighborhoods and to the needs of the people. They can't afford to become insulated from the people around them, or they close within months.

As new congregations grow, they provide streams of leadership also adept in reaching the unchurched. Many future church planters experience their call to ministry as laypersons in new churches. New churches become excellent resources for planting other churches. Reaching younger and more diverse populations, providing future leadership, multiplying missional impact, starting other churches, and returning financial strength to the conference—these are the multiple long-term consequences that make starting new congregations an essential lever for change.

The Gathering in St. Louis began when an associate pastor approached the superintendent and bishop with his desire to start a congregation. He formed a leadership team and identified a mission field while remaining on staff and using the larger church as his base. The superintendent negotiated with a small congregation that had declined to eighteen attendees and was ideally located for the new start. The church closed, and the new congregation renovated the facility. The congregation thrived by reaching younger adults with a passion for urban life, a taste for blended/traditional worship, a love for Christ, and a desire to serve the city and the world. When attendance reached six hundred, the pastor of a smaller church rethinking its future initiated conversations with The Gathering, and soon the young church expanded to two worship sites. Last Easter, The Gathering led worship at four sites. Average attendance now surpasses one thousand people. The Gathering has become a center point for mission, with hundreds of people engaged in hands-on projects. One Christmas Eve, they received more than $111,000, and the next year they received $155,000, which they contributed entirely to Kingdom House, a United Methodist urban ministry, and to building water wells in Mozambique.

The story of Morning Star Church in St. Charles parallels The Gathering. Approaching its fifteenth year, Morning Star worships with 2,100 people, has started two new congregations, provides a stream of pastors and lay leadership for conference projects, attracts talented staff to Missouri, teaches other congregations, and gives more than 100 percent of its apportionments each year.

No lever influences the future of a conference more than an effective strategy for planting new churches. If you're going to use a lever, reach for a big one!

"Go To" Instincts

Jesus sent the disciples out "to every city and place he was about to go" (Luke 10:1). He commissioned his followers to "go and make disciples of all nations" (Matt 28:19). In the book of Acts, the Holy Spirit weaves people from all places into a living community, the church. The people of God attended worship together, broke bread, learned from the disciples, and shared as anyone had need (Acts 2:42-47). Peter and the early Christians carried the message of Christ throughout the Jewish world, forming faith communities. Paul started churches across the Mediterranean. Forming faith communities and planting churches is a missional strategy from our earliest roots.

This outward focus derives from our theology of grace. When we speak of God's grace, we highlight the gift-like quality of God's love. God loves us with an everlasting love, a love that is unearned, unachieved, and unmerited. The word *grace* also emphasizes the active quality of God's love. God's love is a searching love, a seeking love, a pursuing love. In Jesus' parables, shepherds search for sheep, women look for coins, fathers eagerly anticipate reconciliation. Jesus travels from place to place, stepping across social boundaries, speaking with forbidden foreigners, entering the homes of tax collectors, reaching out to lepers, interceding on behalf of the woman accused of adultery. Jesus reveals the grace of God, and grace pushes, propels, compels, interrupts, drives, motivates, and takes us to new places and new people. Grace drives us outward beyond the walls of our church and stretches us beyond the concerns of our community. Grace never sits still.

John Wesley and the early Methodists realized that to go to every city and place Jesus intended to go meant reaching people unreached by the church of their day. He offended the sensibilities of church leaders when he experimented with field preaching to reach the laborers and the poor. He formed classes, bands, and societies and founded chapels and preaching houses to take the gift of God's grace to the most remote areas. Mobilized by God's grace, early Methodists visited prisons, ministered with the poor, fed the hungry, educated children, and addressed the social evils of the era.

The whole Wesleyan system was designed for expansion. The circuits that worked well in England for forming faith communities across broad swaths of territory with minimal resources worked with extraordinary effectiveness in America. Circuit riders covered entire states, forming faith communities in farm houses, trading posts, and emerging communities. Clergy started churches, laity started churches, and churches started churches.

Methodism began with "go to" instincts, but has become a "come to" denomination. Our passivity is a recent phenomenon. Waiting passively for people to find us, to come to us, and to like our way of doing things betrays our Methodist roots and Wesleyan theology. Planting faith communities to reach people with the message of Christ should be an absolute expectation. Church planting seems new, difficult, countercultural, and exceptional when formerly it was natural, expected, and nonnegotiable. The case for developing a conference strategy derives from the mission of Christ, our theology of grace, our Wesleyan roots, and our passion for helping others grow in grace and in the knowledge and love of God.

Some conferences operate with a well-tuned, effective strategy for planting churches, and we can learn from them. But some conferences plant churches in haphazard, inconsistent ways without systems for preparation, supervision, or evaluation. Each church plant becomes a separate and unrelated experience, with no consistent streams to supply leaders or funding. Some conferences unintentionally become good at starting small, struggling, unsustainable congregations that they can't close without assuming massive debt.

A conference strategy for new church starts doesn't mean adopting a lengthy study paper outlining a complex linear organizational process or merely listing unrealistic aspirations. A strategy establishes a priority, defines an objective, mobilizes people, and aligns resources. A strategy is simple, clear, and succinct and focuses attention toward desired outcomes. It fosters system-wide planning.

Without defined strategies, conference leaders feel frustrated and say things like, "I don't know if I have permission to pursue this conversation or not. I don't know whether this fits the strategy." Wasted energy, lost time, and underperformance result from having no strategies. No one knows what to work on.

With a strategy, everyone knows, "We are actively and assertively looking for opportunities to start churches, and we welcome any ideas for recruiting people, identifying locations, developing funds, or forming partnerships." With a strategy, people begin to work on the tactics—the distinct steps and methods for achieving the end—each from his or her own position of leadership. A strategy guides work for everyone, including the cabinet, the finance committee, the trustees, and the conference as a whole. A strategy sets direction, aligns energy, and moves the project forward.

Leadership Streams

One challenge in a strategy for planting churches is the difficulty in identifying persons with the particular gifts that predict success in this specialized ministry. How can we improve the stream of people with the particular calling, talents, and energy to start congregations?

Formerly, the conference subjectively identified "entrepreneurial" pastors, mostly extraverts who easily formed relationships and risk-takers comfortable with uncharted territory. We selected one or two such people each year and sent them to the New Church Leadership Institute (NCLI) sponsored by the jurisdiction for five days of training. Then they were assigned to plant a church. The system worked moderately well, but this approach provided only a limited stream of pastors. Because of the subjectivity of the selection process, nearly all persons identified were young, white males with a particular temperament. The tactic created a bottleneck for finding people.

Seven years ago, we changed tactics. We began to send fifteen to twenty people each year to the NCLI, whether we thought they had the gifts for planting churches or not. The practices learned at NCLI enhanced ministry for everyone. Mentor pastors, superintendents, and the Director of Congregational Excellence attended NCLI to observe, listen, and search for those pastors who responded with passion and gifts. Each year four or five people emerge as prospects for starting churches, and several others sort themselves out by expressing reservations about planting churches. The list of candidates became more diverse, which has allowed us to successfully appoint increasing numbers of women and ethnic pastors to plant churches as well as pastors from varying clergy statuses and ages that we might otherwise have overlooked with our previous tactic. Forty percent of our participants in NCLI are female, and more clergywomen plant churches in Missouri than in any other conference in the jurisdiction. We started three predominantly African American congregations, a number of Hispanic congregations, and several intentionally multiethnic congregations using pastors identified through NCLI.

After a few years, the tactic deepened. The seventy pastors who had attended NCLI demonstrated greater understanding of church dynamics and were more likely to maintain an outward focus, even in traditional congregations, and so we began to send nearly all our beginning full-time pastors as well as newly appointed superintendents. NCLI provides a practicum in evangelism and in demographics that benefits any pastor.

And we use NCLI to recruit seminary students and pastors from other conferences who feel disillusioned by their own conference's unwillingness or inability to plant churches. We pay their way to NCLI, based on the belief that the training contributes to effectiveness wherever they eventually serve. The stream widened and grew stronger. Success fosters success, and the network of young pastors feeling called to plant churches is well connected. We received more inquiries and began to communicate and cooperate with more conferences to train and transfer talented people.

Our own churches also feed the stream of potential church planters, especially large congregations and new churches. A congregation hires a layperson for a staff position who later seeks candidacy and licensing as a local pastor while continuing to serve on staff. Some set their sights on seminary and ordination. We support nontraditional career development paths and encourage our large churches to do this. This stream provides leaders with a proven track record of fruitfulness and experience in a growing church—two rare attributes that are particularly useful for planting churches.

These tactics represent the front door of the leadership development system. We've widened it so that we identify more candidates. When we discern whether to assign someone to plant a particular church, another phase begins that involves intense assessments with the Director of Congregational Excellence, the executive assistant, the superintendent, and a member from the Congregational Development Team. Interviews focus on gifts, temperament, experience, family support, psychological health, work style, fruitfulness, and affinity to the mission field. We focus on their actual experience in initiating ministry, starting groups, inviting strangers, and leading teams. Pastors who plant churches don't step into an existing system; they create one, and so we explore organizational skill. We assess four to six people a year and then appoint three or four to start new churches.

After we appoint pastors to start churches, we send them to the "New Church Start Boot Camp" for church planters. They receive one week of intensive preparation, learning the logistics and practicalities for forming leadership teams, meeting people, and finding locations, among other skills.

Upon their completion of the "Boot Camp," we weave them into the network of church planters in our conference, and they fall under the supervision of the Director of Congregational Excellence. Benchmarks are mutually agreed upon, and planters are given continued access to the director, executive assistant, and a coach for support, encouragement, and problem solving. No matter what challenge they face, they always have a phone number to call for help.

As a congregation becomes self-sufficient, we ask the pastor to help us identify other potential leaders, and the cycle begins again.

In the last six years, six female and twenty-three male pastors have been assigned to start new churches, including four African Americans, twenty-two whites, two Hispanics, and one Pacific Islander, using lay pastors, local pastors, provisional elders, and elders of all ages.

What's your system for providing a stream of leadership gifted in planting churches? What are the steps and phases? What role do various leaders play in sustaining the system? What are the bottlenecks, and how do you address them?

Funding Streams

Funding is a second bottleneck that limits a strategy for starting churches. Church plants are capital intensive. They require start-up costs for salary, benefits, and administrative expenses before any revenue exists from within the congregation. An assertive conference strategy includes plans for deepening and widening streams of support.

We established the goal of planting three new congregations a year for the next ten years. In our experience, a church start requires $300,000 during a three-year period before the congregation reaches self-sustainability.

This means that the Missouri Conference must find $900,000 a year, not including recruitment, training, or supervisory costs or the salaries for the Director of Congregational Excellence and staff. Where will this come from? We also want to reduce financial pressures on congregations by limiting apportionments. If we apportion all the costs for an ambitious church start strategy, we find ourselves closing churches faster than we plant them because of the added financial burden!

We highlight the priority for starting new churches by giving visible support through our conference budget. The conference funds one new church a year from the budget.

Look at chart A, and imagine that each square represents a church we intend to start during the next ten years at a rate of three per year. Each of the thirty squares represents our need for $300,000. If the conference budget funds one church plant per year through apportionments, then we can check off ten of the boxes. Those boxes are lettered CB for conference budget. We're one-third of the way to our goal. Where do we find other funding?

Chart A

	1	2	3
Year 1	CB	MF	
Year 2	CB		
Year 3	CB		
Year 4	CB	MF	
Year 5	CB		
Year 6	CB		
Year 7	CB	MF	
Year 8	CB		
Year 9	CB		
Year 10	CB	MF	

Chart B

	1	2	3
Year 1	CB	MF	PD
Year 2	CB	CC	PP
Year 3	CB	PD	
Year 4	CB	MF	PP
Year 5	CB		CC
Year 6	CB	PD	PP
Year 7	CB	MF	
Year 8	CB	CC	PP
Year 9	CB		PD
Year 10	CB	MF	PP

We search for alternative streams, knowing that some are reliable and ongoing, and others will prove sporadic and unpredictable. For one stream, we work with the Missouri United Methodist Foundation, whose primary mission is helping congregations establish endowment funds, manage investment assets, and encourage long-term giving through estate planning and planned giving. The foundation provides scholarships for seminary students and grants for local church projects. The annual grants total several hundred thousand dollars. These grants help congregations, enhance the visibility of the foundation, and foster positive relationships with the conference.

As the Missouri conference became clear about its priorities, we collaborated with the foundation on key strategies to explore how the mission of the foundation interweaves with that of the conference. The more clearly we expressed our priorities, the more interested the foundation became in helping. As the conference aligned its resources, this stimulated the foundation to modify its grant process to address congregational excellence and pastoral excellence. The foundation continues to provide scholarships and local church grants at helpful levels, but they also aggregate grants into a larger gift to the conference to support new church starts and clergy excellence. The bishop meets with their board each year to articulate priorities, and the Director of Congregational Excellence and executive assistant report regularly on progress with church planting. For several years now, gifts have extended up to $100,000 per year. The foundation has made no binding commitments, but we will continue to nurture this collaboration. An annual $100,000 gift fills one square on our chart every three years. (See chart A, the boxes marked MF for Methodist Foundation.) Clarity and accountability attract collaboration.

We still require other streams for our plan to work. Many laypersons have a vision for United Methodism larger than their local church, and they possess the financial resources to give beyond their congregations. We formed Pathways Partners as a forum for the bishop to articulate the vision for Missouri United Methodism directly with potential donors, and to solicit their counsel and support. A pastor coordinates Pathways Partners, providing communication and event planning. The bishop meets with potential donors to discuss strategies and answer questions. Participants complete pledge cards or request personal conversations about larger gifts. We've expanded to include ways for congregations to give. The annual funding support generated by Pathways Partners has totaled about $150,000 for the last four years. On chart B, we can now fill in a box every other year with PP for Pathways Partners. We have now filled two-thirds of the boxes.

Word reached one wealthy donor who prefers not to attend Pathways Partners meetings but who passionately supports the strategy of starting new churches. The bishop met with him personally, and the Director for Congregational Excellence keeps him informed about our work. He supports with an annual gift of $100,000, or one church plant every three years. On chart B, we've added his contribution as PD, personal donation.

A less consistent stream of support comes from selling property after closing churches. Working in collaboration with the conference chancellor, the treasurer, and the cabinet, we developed a system to initiate conversations with congregations who reach the final stages of their ministry in order to make critical decisions about property and resources before their buildings become liabilities. Every few years, the sale of a property generates enough revenue that we can channel those resources toward new church starts. On chart B, church closings are marked by CC.

Chart B shows all the squares completed except for four. The support from most streams—the Missouri Foundation, Pathways Partners, personal donors, and church closings—comes with no guarantees. These streams require hard work, continuing cultivation, critical collaboration, credible accountability, and the attention of the bishop, directors, and lay leaders to see these through. But the chart establishes a direction, forms a plan, and undergirds a strategy for funding. Without the generosity of donors, no plan can succeed. Without a clear strategy, donors have nothing to give to.

The greatest new stream for funding is literally *off the charts*! It's the conference's growing collaboration with existing churches who want to start congregations. We invite healthy growing congregations to work with us to identify potential sites, personnel, and opportunities. We work closely with these partners, assuring that any initiative remains consistent with the mission of that church, has considerable pastoral and lay support, uses conference processes for identifying planters, follows conference benchmarks, and relates to the Director of Congregational Excellence. In some circumstances, the local congregation accepts the entire cost of starting a church; in others, the conference supports at one-third or one-half the usual costs.

Setting large congregations free to plant churches or to initiate partnerships with declining congregations in their mission field dramatically changes the funding puzzle.

A congregation from another conference launched a new church in our conference, and then funded a restart when another church floundered. More than 1,500 people now worship at those two sites. A rural church established a Hispanic congregation, sharing the costs with the conference. A church in St. Charles envisions planting one new church every other year.

Look again at chart B and the four unfunded openings. If we were to write CS (for congregationally sponsored) for all the plans underway to collaborate and cost share with churches who voluntarily plant churches, we fill the remaining blank squares, and we can add another column as we anticipate starting more than three a year. This year we launched six new churches.

What are your funding streams? What's a realistic goal for future new church starts?

Are there congregations ready and able to help? Do they have permission?

Buffering and Interpreting

A conference strategy also addresses a third limiting factor, the resistance from existing congregations, pastors, and laity toward new churches.

In its more passive forms, resistance surfaces as an unwillingness to align resources, redirect funds, reconfigure budgets, or support staff positions to supervise new church starts. Conferences with $10 million operating budgets conclude that they have no money available for starting churches. Is the critical issue a shortage of resources, or resistance to shifting priorities?

People express resistance in statements such as these:

You can't let them do that! The "them" is any church launching a second site or relocating, any congregation repurposing an abandoned church, or a church planter identifying a location for worship. The "that" to which people object is offering alternative worship, utilizing marketing and social media techniques, launching high-impact mission initiatives, using nontraditional venues, and reaching the unchurched. In short, the criticism is aimed at exactly those missional instincts and behaviors we need most!

New churches rob members from our churches. Most United Methodists support the notion of starting new congregations in general, but fear the consequences of planting a church in their area. In fact, a new church start seldom interrupts existing worship trends of nearby congregations. Existing churches that were growing continue to grow and those that were declining continue to decline. New churches attract age, economic, ethnic, or lifestyle niches of the population that existing congregations miss. They attract people whom existing churches never reach.

Why can't the conference send the money to our struggling church rather than starting a new church? The existing congregation has had a hundred years to reach the population around it. It's time to give someone else a chance with a fresh approach.

New churches get all the attention. Focusing on new churches doesn't diminish the essential ministry of existing congregations. Newborns in a household require more attention than their older siblings, and teenagers demand more time than they will when they become self-sufficient.

Existing churches received extra attention during their early years, too. As the saying goes, "It takes a village to raise a child." Starting new congregations requires the attention and encouragement of other congregations.

It's only about growth and institutional survival. No, it's about the mission of the church and faithfulness to Christ. New churches reach people with the gift and demand of God's grace that we won't reach any other way. Your church was once a new church start, and the difference it has made in your life and the life of your community isn't merely about institutional survival.

New churches don't feel Methodist, they don't use the hymnal, and theologically they're not mainline. This generalization simply isn't true. Some of the fastest growing new churches adhere closely to Wesleyan theology and demonstrate worship styles ranging from traditional to edgy. John Wesley and the early Methodists faced these same allegations. New congregations aren't for us; they are for others. They reach next generations, people with no church background, and diverse populations that we never reach by adhering to our own personal preferences.

Leaders must attend to such fears without allowing resistance to restrain them in this essential task. A strategy for new churches draws as many people into the work as possible, and this requires active listening, excellent communication, a clearly articulated vision, and entry places for people who want to help. A strategy requires interpreters—intermediaries who articulate the vision in general or who can describe the plan for a particular start in compelling and inviting ways. Interpreters act as buffers.

A larger church expressed interest in establishing a second site utilizing the property of a church that had declined to sixty people led by a part-time, retired pastor. The facility carried a $1.5 million debt. The congregation could no longer make payments. We closed the smaller church and reopened it under the name of the larger church a few months later. Area pastors were anxious about the plan. I met with them and listened to their concerns, answered questions, and confirmed the intention to move forward.

Fear distorts vision, and lack of communication feeds fear. The pastors asked reasonable questions, but the underlying emotional field screamed, "You can't do that. What about us?" I asked them to assess our alternatives and their likely outcomes. If we don't approve this partnership, a community of sixty people will suffer to a bitter end and scatter to the wind, the bank will foreclose, and the conference will assume the liability. If we support the proposal, experienced volunteers will lead ministries under the leadership of a full-time pastor, the resources of the larger church will subsume the debt, and we anticipate a worshipping community of 250 people. Which outcome is consistent with our mission? Every pastor desired the second alternative, but fear bends us toward decisions that would lead to the first.

Leaders in The United Methodist Church today must have a high threshold for pain. They absorb the disillusionment and sorrow of many people experiencing loss as their churches age and decline. Exciting new adventures seem remote and unreal. Grief displays all its natural shades, including denial, blame, and anger on its way to acceptance and new life. Unexamined grief causes otherwise good people to sabotage effective strategies for change.

A strategy for planting churches involves bringing pastors and laity together a year or more in advance when the conference identifies an area for launching new work. Leaders answer questions, relieve fears, and clarify purposes. They also identify partners, allies, sponsoring congregations, and those wanting to collaborate. The success or failure of new churches belongs to all of us.

Fresh Approaches and Innovative Models

Thirty years ago, conferences bought five acres, assigned a pastor, and supplied three years of salary. After this "parachute drop," church planters were on their own—little training, few resources, no mentors, minimal support from area churches, and no specialized supervision.

Fifteen years ago, two or three other models emerged, including "mother-daughter" models (a large church gives birth to a new and different church), and "second sites" (a church operates in two locations with the same name, pastor, staff, and mission).

Today, a whole host of new approaches and experiments are underway, and a healthy conference strategy places a premium on initiative and experimentation.

In addition to the parachute drop, mother-daughter, and second site, we find the following models:

Across Conference Bounds. Rez Downtown is one of two congregations started in the Missouri Conference by Church of the Resurrection from the Great Plains Conference. The pastor serves under the supervision of the larger church and is a member of the other conference. We adjusted the trust clause so that if the church closes, the assets return to the founding congregation rather than to our conference. The

Missouri apportionment formula applies, and membership and other statistics accrue to Missouri. A thousand rules and considerations could have stopped these projects going forward, including conflicts over who supervises, who evaluates, who superintends, who pays, which conference do members attend, and whose church development director oversees. By beginning with the end in mind (we will make this work!), we've overcome every obstacle and have now begun conversations for a Missouri church to start a congregation in another conference using a similar pattern.

Church within a Church. Broadway UMC in Kansas City continued its traditional worship while inviting a new church plant within its facility to offer a completely different worship style for a different target population.

Multiple Sites with Streaming Video. Congregations offer alternative venues with musical and liturgical leadership but with a live feed of the sermon from the central church.

Community Café. The Union Café in Dallas is a coffee shop outreach ministry that forms community and provides support and service to a mostly student population.

Restarts. The conference closes a struggling congregation that has a useful facility, lets the building sit dormant, and then remodels the building and reshapes the leadership before restarting under a different name.

Repurposing Abandoned Buildings. The conference starts congregations in former UMC facilities by renovating, renaming, and appointing a church-start pastor.

Closing Two to Start One. Two rural congregations struggling to pay full-time pastors purposefully closed, celebrating their rich histories. Both pastors were assigned to other churches. After a few months, the conference started a new church, attracting about one-third of its initial attendance from one former church and one-third from the other. The other third were new people. The congregation, Trinity UMC near Piedmont, Missouri, has thrived.

House Churches. We've experimented with appointing a licensed local pastor to start a house group in one of our rural districts with the intention of training leadership so that the pastor eventually coordinates ten weekly gatherings in homes for prayer, worship, and teaching.

Recovery Churches. Conferences have launched faith communities focused on the special needs of the recovery community, giving hope and support to recovering alcoholics, drug addicts, or problem gamblers.

Sponsored Congregations. Two of our new churches and one of our restarts focus on the urban poor. They surpass attendance benchmarks, but they never become financially self-sustaining. We've joined two of the churches to other congregations. In the third, we solicit sponsors, inviting area congregations and individuals to pledge support.

Immigrant Initiatives. We've cooperated with Wesleyan judicatories not directly related to The United Methodist Church to provide pastoral support in native languages.

Online Communities. A number of congregations have as many people "attending" services online or downloading podcasts as they have present in worship, and they're experimenting with online communities.

These examples represent a sampling of the many models for forming faith communities. These require recruiting leadership differently, by drawing from a variety of elders, local pastors, lay ministers, and laity. Many of these new expressions have emerged precisely because our traditional approaches have been too costly, too slow, and too encumbered by bureaucracy.

In the flat world, collaboration is faster, farther, wider, and deeper than ever before. The church planting conversation is rich, vigorous, and varied. A vast literature and several parachurch events support starting new churches, and church planters across boundaries readily connect and collaborate. Conferences must tap into the larger network.

Too many of our systems operate with the default of "You can't do that because, or until . . ." Can we instead develop the instinct to say *Yes*, and then shape the conversation in a manner that reduces risk, increases the likelihood of success, and maintains faithfulness to our mission?

Everyone Has a Role

Everyone has a role in a conference strategy for starting new churches. Establishing a priority means the job doesn't rest with one person. In a system that distributes authority as diffusely as The United Methodist Church, clear priorities give direction to everyone, and asks them to consider, "What's my contribution?"

In the Missouri Conference, the Director of Congregational Excellence carries the portfolio for new church starts. The director relates to a congregational development team comprised of laity and clergy with particular expertise or experience with church planting or church growth. The director's executive assistant collects and evaluates reports and oversees accounts and expenses for each church plant. The director serves on the cabinet and participates in appointive conversations, particularly as it relates to church planters. The director has direct access to the bishop. The director recruits, trains, evaluates, and supervises new church pastors, and collaborates with superintendents to identify personnel, locations, and opportunities.

The bishop articulates the purpose and priority of starting new churches in teaching, writing, clergy gatherings, and preaching. The episcopal address at annual conference refers to the goals, funding, progress, and setbacks. The bishop reports each six months to the episcopacy committee. The bishop solicits funding and interprets the work for conference boards. For cross-conference plans or innovative experiments, the bishop focuses on outcomes so that regulations in the *Book of Discipline* don't impede leaders from acting. The bishop helps the Director of Congregational Excellence succeed.

Superintendents work collaboratively with the Director of Congregational Excellence to identify sites, personnel, and resources. They support the director's supervision for church planters while maintaining their own responsibility according to the *Discipline*. They interpret the value and priority of new church starts. They attend training for church planters, and they prepare district mission strategies using demographics to identify underserved areas.

The lay leader champions the strategy for various boards, councils, committees, and public events. Lay Leadership Development groups focus on teaching growth strategies to laity across the conference.

Other conference directors regularly collaborate with the Director of Congregational Excellence, helping to solicit funding, hosting events, or problem solving obstacles. The treasurer works with the director on issues related to salary, grants, apportionments, gifts, and training expenses.

The Mission Council (our conference council), CFA, and the trustees work cooperatively to support church starts. The Mission Council receives regular updates, CFA gives priority funding, and the trustees channel funds that result from selling property toward new churches.

Many of the best ideas come from pastors and laity in local congregations. New church starts is the research and development branch of the conference, an area that attracts the interest of many creative and passionate leaders. Pastors and laity identify opportunities, start conversations, and contact their superintendent.

53

Failures and Successes

We've learned much about developing a conference strategy for new church starts. As usual, we learn perhaps as much from our failures as we do from our successes. What follows is a list of principles drawn from our experience.

There are several bad reasons to start a new church. These include motives such as the following: 1) The strategy calls for three new churches a year and we've only started two; 2) For egalitarian reasons, such as, "We've started one in all the other districts, so we have to plant one in this district"; 3) We need to create an appointment for a pastor because of an oversupply of clergy; 4) We must mollify the demands or complaints of a sponsoring congregation; 5) We must save a historic building or a dying church.

Use benchmarks. Adjust them if circumstances merit it, but maintain high expectations. We don't need more struggling, dependent, unsustainable congregations.

Failure is inevitable. Expect it, plan for it, and clearly communicate the risks. Starting churches is high risk. To move from a 50 percent success rate to a 66 percent rate has taken phenomenal training, collaboration, learning, and a talented Director of Congregational Excellence.

Church planters need reassurance that failure won't damage their careers. If they have done their best, responded to coaching, and worked hard, their careers aren't at risk.

Fail quickly. If efforts to start a church aren't working, stop doing it. Give the director the authority to close down churches that don't meet benchmarks.

Create a system that improves with failure. In some conferences, each failure makes other failures more likely because of lost trust and support. In other conferences, each failure makes other failures less likely because leaders assess, learn, and correct.

The greatest predictor of failure is the uncoachable pastor. If the pastor stops seeking help and asking questions, becomes isolated, fails to participate in support groups, and doesn't return calls to coaches, then remove the pastor immediately.

Identifying locations has become increasingly difficult. City councils and developers no longer think churches add value to a neighborhood, and building managers don't want to lease to churches because neighbors complain.

Transferring church planters from other conferences entails risk. The decision to do so requires considerable due diligence, reference checks, and background screening.

Our models don't fit immigrant populations. We learn the most from other denominations or affiliate Wesleyan churches.

Mergers seldom work, unless done with extraordinary care. It is more successful to close and restart after several months with different leadership than to merge congregations.[2]

Never coerce large churches into starting churches to solve conference problems. Rescuing churches, saving buildings, or providing an appointment are unsatisfactory reasons to ask churches to start congregations. Congregational initiatives must fit their *congregation's* mission.

Training modules for forming new faith communities become obsolete quickly. This happens because of the rapid changes in attitudes, values, and behaviors of young people. Don't get stuck in old models.

Moderate the expectations of pastors. Pastors considered for starting churches get their hopes up and feel deflated when they are appointed to an existing congregation instead.

New churches benefit from specialized supervision by those who have successfully started congregations themselves. Sharing supervisory responsibilities between the specialist and the superintendent requires intentional communication and collaboration, or conflicts will arise.

Conferences and congregations must listen to next generations. They know what works and can lead us.

Strategies and Tactics

A strategy for starting congregations provides an extraordinary lever for influencing the direction and mission of a conference. No legacy could be more important for the mission of Christ than ensuring a future of outward-focused faith communities.

Every conference should have a strategy for starting churches. Tactics, however, differ from conference to conference. The details on how to organize, identify leadership, find funding, coordinate with the cabinet, align resources, and evaluate the new church are all tactics that support the strategy. Tactics change, sometimes rapidly. They multiply, deepen, and expand, or they don't work, and we abandon them to explore other tactics.

The tactics above uniquely serve the Missouri Conference. The lesson to take away isn't which tactics to use but the importance of having a robust strategy owned by the conference, supported by its leaders, and with sufficient direction that people will work out the tactics most applicable to their context.

And yet, we can't "new church start" ourselves out of decline. An effective strategy for new church starts works in tandem with systems to strengthen pastoral leadership and to intervene in existing congregations. The second lever addresses clergy peer learning, the most effective way of enhancing leadership in a conference.

Conversation Questions

Describe some ways your life has been shaped by belonging to a congregation. How has God used a congregation to change you, mold you, and call you?

How was your congregation started, and when? What role did the conference or other churches play in planting your congregation and providing leadership for it?

How familiar are you with the systems by which your conference recruits and prepares pastors to plant new congregations? What particular gifts and leadership qualities are required?

What alternative streams of financial support does your conference use to support new church starts?

How well does your conference do with starting new faith communities and encouraging congregations to do so? How can decisions by conferences foster life in Christ for more and more people? How actively does your own congregation support such efforts?

If every congregation supported the starting of new congregations as avidly as your congregation does, would your conference be starting more or fewer congregations?

How has your congregation helped start a congregation? What role could you play to support new church starts?

Who is your congregation uniquely qualified and perfectly situated to reach whom no one else can possibly reach? What creative alternative approaches to planting a church might work best in your context?

Visit a church that has started during the last five years. If one hasn't been started by your conference, visit a new church planted by another denomination or another conference. How are new churches different from established congregations? How does the new church reach people whom your congregation can't reach?

The Second Lever

A STRATEGY FOR CLERGY PEER LEARNING

Developing a strategy for clergy peer learning is the second lever. Leading a congregation is a unique calling, requiring relational, organizational, supervisory, financial, marketing, and business skills, as well as theological training, spiritual grounding, and the ability to pray, preach, counsel, teach, and mobilize people. Congregations need someone not only to love them but also to lead them. With the rapidly changing contexts in which we serve, learning these skills and deepening these gifts requires lifelong learning. Clergy learn best from other clergy.

The challenge for a conference is how to draw clergy into the optimal setting for learning leadership and deepening the practices that lead churches to expand their ministry and reach more people for the purposes of Christ.

Considerable research supports the effectiveness of clergy peer-learning groups. The Lilly Endowment, Alban Institute, Duke Divinity School, Texas Methodist Foundation, and other researchers and consultants substantiate that even a mediocre clergy peer-learning group shapes pastoral behavior and identity more than the best workshops, lectures, or books. Nothing influences clergy leadership more than a supportive learning community of other pastors.

A comprehensive study by Austin Presbyterian Seminary funded by the Lilly Endowment researched whether peer-group involvement makes a difference in clergy leadership and how peer learning affects the congregations the clergy serve.[1] Pastors who regularly participate in peer learning are more likely to promote a culture of involvement that actively assimilates newcomers and fully involves members. In addition, those pastors more actively lead their congregations to devote effort to community service and youth ministry. The length of time clergy have participated in peer groups strongly correlates with numerical growth in the congregation. Belonging to a peer group legitimizes activities that many pastors intuitively know are necessary for a vital ministry, causing them to give more time to essential practices.[2] Clergy peer learning changes pastors and changes the churches they serve.

The research matches my personal experience. I've belonged to numerous covenant, peer mentoring, and accountability groups; and from my earliest years in ministry, I've participated in lectionary groups or clergy brown-bag lunches. These groups provided counsel and encouragement, and they reminded me that I wasn't alone in the challenges I faced. Pastors understand pastors.

Even today, my most valuable learning community is a semiannual gathering of ten active bishops who pray for one another, learn together, discuss a common reading, and explore case studies that focus on real life challenges we face in our work.

Conscientious pastors seek such support or create mentoring relationships with other clergy on their own initiative. They know that leaders need allies, confidants, and colleagues and that they can't go it alone. They develop peer-learning opportunities for themselves.

But many pastors participate in such groups sporadically, even though they know the benefits of continuous peer learning. Many informal peer groups lack focus, consistency, or intentionality. These groups don't help pastors master new skills for ministry. Without proper boundaries, meetings deteriorate into gripe sessions and rumormongering or strong personalities dominate with their personal agendas.

Clergy peer learning provides the most advantageous setting when it has focus, consistency, quality, and healthy leadership. A purposeful peer-learning system fundamentally shifts how we learn the practice of ministry. We know this works.

The Way Jesus Taught Us to Learn

Jesus taught us to learn in community. He traveled with a community and taught in groups. He sent his disciples two by two so they would serve as resources of support and accountability for each other. The work pastors perform is fundamentally countercultural, and they need colleagues who understand their mission and encourage their effort.

Jesus said, "I am the vine; you are the branches. If you remain in me and I in you, then you will produce much fruit. Without me, you can't do anything." (John 15:5). Regular engagement with our clergy sisters and brothers keeps us connected with the vine and focused on the fruit of changed lives and a transformed world.

Wesley developed powerful tools for forming community. He organized people into classes, bands, and societies to hold each other accountable for growth in grace and to foster active service. These became places to learn faith and to practice teaching, preaching, and leading. Small groups feed leadership streams.

What happens in a peer-learning group?

Belonging to a clergy peer-learning group has the effect of pulling each person out of his or her immediate situation to give a larger view, a slightly more universal perspective. Each topic, whether guided by a book or brought by someone facing a particular challenge, draws every pastor up onto a balcony to view situations from a fresh perspective.

For instance, a pastor may face the challenge of supervising an ineffective youth director who is nevertheless well liked by members. How does the pastor navigate this dilemma without causing undue conflict? Can the pastor survive the reaction if the youth director is let go? Such a challenge inevitably strikes a pastor as relevant. As each pastor mulls over the situation, he or she thinks about a choir director, a custodian, or a volunteer who presents a similar challenge. Can a pastor ever "fire" a volunteer? The peer group processes alternatives. They point to resources that can help. Perhaps they offer no clear answers, but they all feel more confident, connected, and empowered by the knowledge that what they face isn't unique. "Without guidance, a people will fall, but there is victory with many counselors" (Prov 11:14).

Each time the participants leave a session, they feel encouraged to try things they were fearful to do before. They nudge each other into better decisions and bolder ministry.

In peer learning, we become to each other the voice of Christ's encouragement, invitation, and accountability. Dietrich Bonheoffer reminds us that we see "in the companionship of a fellow Christian a physical sign of the presence of Christ."[3] The Christ in one's own heart is weaker than the Christ in the word of a brother or sister.

The benefit of sifting through experiences with colleagues goes beyond learning organizational theories or gleaning helpful hints. Each person learns something relevant to his or her journey and growth as a pastor and follower of Christ. Pastors receive a wider perspective on the world in which they work, love, play, and serve. As meaning is unlocked by one person on a topic, an overflowing of insight connects to other persons at an interior level. The Spirit of God works through the conversation, weaving, binding, healing, correcting, reminding.

And by the grace of God, with consistent participation with our peers, certain attributes of leadership are sharpened and deepened. We lead the followers of Christ with more courage, more clarity, more patience, and a greater resolve to focus the attentions of the church outward to the world. God uses our colleagues to gently and persistently shape us, like a potter forming clay.

Pastors overestimate their capacity to handle challenges all by themselves, and they underestimate the power of community to help. Belonging to a supportive learning community keeps them connected, rooted, grounded. Community helps them break through the paralysis that comes when they face resistance or conflict. Peers lend hope.

Toward a Strategy

A strategy for drawing clergy into peer-learning groups began for us by evaluating the tools already in place. Which learning experiences already underway do we foster, which do we leave alone, which do we allow to fade away? What new models might we offer that address unmet needs?

Many clergy already participated in lectionary groups, weekly lunches, ecumenical meetings, or other self-organized, informal gatherings. Some participated in covenant groups, with a spiritual formation focus.

Missouri held an annual Ministers' School, three days of lectures from guest speakers using a traditional model inherited from the 1960s. Topics and presentations varied widely in purpose, quality, relevance, and interest. Attendance had been declining for years.

The conference offered sporadic events, again with mixed quality but more focused on topics relevant to pastors, such as staff development, capital fund drives, stewardship, and other practical skills. Some events targeted affinity groups, such as pastors of urban churches or large congregations. Our earliest tactics involved increasing the quality and frequency of these events and giving high-functioning congregations the green light to initiate training for pastors and congregations.

While the conference searched for models to reach more leaders, a group of pastors formed to consider how to learn and teach best practices and adapted a plan they read about in Paul Borden's *Hit the Bullseye*.[4] These pastors committed to nine monthly meetings of four hours, and they agreed to read a common book before each meeting and to ask one of their peers to moderate the meeting. During sessions, the group discussed the assigned reading, and they took turns processing particular challenges experienced in their churches. They prayed for one another, and followed up with one another to offer continuing support.

The experience of these six pastors became the basis of Pastoral Leadership Development (PLD) groups as we elaborated on the model and experimented with ways to increase quality and consistency. PLD groups now form the cornerstone of our conference strategy for clergy peer learning.

Pastoral Leadership Development Groups

Several conferences have experimented with a variety of approaches toward clergy peer learning, and many have seen remarkable success as measured by the effects on clergy morale and leadership development. Pastoral Leadership Development groups became the primary tactic for enhancing clergy leadership skills and fostering collaborative learning for the Missouri Conference. PLD developed into a *sustainable and scalable system for forming high quality, self-directed, voluntary, continuous peer-learning groups that involve the majority of our clergy to focus on the skills for missional, outward-focused ministry*. This chapter highlights having a strategy for clergy peer learning; PLD is merely one tactic in the strategy that we developed for our context. Once again, we aren't suggesting that this tactic will work elsewhere or work best, but we are describing the critical decisions we made and what we learned.

To maintain *quality*, we select, invite, and train PLD leaders from among our most fruitful pastors, peers respected by their colleagues who have led their congregations to greater fruitfulness, regardless of the size or setting of congregations they serve. We compensate leaders for their time with honoraria funded by the registration fees of participants. We coach, train, and retrain peer group leaders. Leaders receive a 190-page facilitator guide that describes the core competencies we want to foster among pastors through PLD. Colleagues don't pretend to be experts. They navigate the same waters daily that all pastors navigate. Peer teachers are fellow learners.

Participation is *voluntary*, and pastors attend because they *want to* and not because they *have to*. We don't want people present who don't want to be there. Nothing drains energy or derails conversation more than people who don't value the experience or who push their own agenda. PLD isn't a place to gripe, blame, undermine, or sabotage. Critical evaluation and feedback are welcome, but people attend to learn and contribute.

To maintain high participation on a voluntary basis requires a premium on excellence. We strive to offer events so well done that those choosing not to participate feel that they've missed something important.

As the number of PLD groups grew from one to five to dozens, the Director of Congregational Excellence worked with a curriculum writer to prepare *a common curriculum*. The 160-page PLD handbook includes a chapter for each of the nine monthly sessions, with questions to focus conversations. The curriculum evolves from year to year as the readings cover a range of topics related to leadership, organizations, social trends, theological reflection, and personal temperament. Each session includes time to process specific issues brought by members. Even with a common curriculum, the actual work is *self-directed*, making it more relevant and contextual.

The curriculum is *skill based* and *mission focused*. This distinguishes PLD from many other clergy peer-learning experiences that focus on spiritual formation, lectionary study, or covenant groups. We encourage participation in such groups, but PLD focuses on sharpening the skills for leading congregations and mobilizing people to fulfill the mission of Christ. PLD helps participants do a better job with the challenges on the pastor's desk every day—worship planning, preaching, supervising staff, budgeting, fund-raising, reaching new people, stimulating mission, moderating conflict, and developing habits for long-term healthy leadership.

All reading adds insight to a pastor's life and work. The particular focus of PLD is how to fulfill the mission of Christ as leaders of congregations. This requires delving into resources with an end in mind. Rather than pursuing their own esoteric interests, participants focus on leading the church. PLD readings don't focus merely on the "how to" of ministry but on understanding systems from a theological perspective. PLD doesn't teach techniques to address only a particular situation; rather it helps pastors learn how to process their way through adaptive challenges with their colleagues and congregations, to grasp underlying dynamics, and to develop the intuition, practices, and collegial resources to lead through any number of challenges.

Pastors anywhere can form PLD groups on their own initiative. The challenge for conferences is how to make the program *scalable*. How does a conference coordinate many such groups for large numbers of pastors while maintaining quality?

Scalability is an unidentified challenge for many United Methodist ministries, and failure to address it limits effectiveness. Many college-age or youth ministries reach a ceiling of twenty-five to thirty-five participants because their model focuses on everyone relating to one central person. Like spokes on a wheel, people connect to the campus minister or youth director at the hub. Such programs can only grow by addition, one person at a time. The challenge is to develop a system that revolves around more than one person or location, with multiple connectors and settings while maintaining the same purpose and quality. Then a ministry grows by multiplication rather than by simple addition.

The conference invited several leaders to join us in developing a scalable model. We included our conference directors, a few pastors and laypersons, and Paul Borden, author of *Hit the Bullseye*. The five expectations we adopted as a conference shaped the conversation as we sought a process that reflected Christ-centeredness, fruitfulness, excellence, accountability, and collaboration. The team deliberated over purpose and content, desired outcomes, communication, invitation, leaders, curriculum, funding, compensation, registration, and the roles of conference staff, superintendents, and district offices. Conferences underestimate the work required to create a scalable plan just as they underestimate the importance of doing so. A scalable plan requires more than one person's part-time, volunteer coordination.

For PLD, scalability meant contracting with many different people to prepare the curriculum, train leadership, lead the groups, identify coaches, register people, assign coaches, and monitor progress. Fewer than five people operate the PLD program, and all of them have many other projects in their portfolios, but several dozen people play a role in teaching, writing, coaching, and evaluating the program. We scale up or size down as participation varies.

As for funding, pastors invest in PLD by paying fees to cover the costs of materials and a nominal honorarium for leaders and coaches. They purchase assigned books on their own. Most participants pay from continuing education allowances or discretionary funds. While group leaders would teach without compensation, they've found the honorarium affirming. When the bishop or a superintendent leads a group, they receive no honorarium. Infrastructure costs, including salaries for directors and staff, fall under the conference budget, and conference funds cover any costs for pastors unable to afford registration fees.

A monthly PLD session includes a welcome, prayer time, a spiritual formation component, and a reminder of the purpose of the gathering. This is followed by an action plan review during which pastors focus on particular challenges they've faced in leading their congregations. The group processes these together, sharing insights and experiences. The facilitator next leads a ninety-minute discussion of the assigned reading. After lunch, the group highlights key learnings and best practices that they've gleaned from the readings, the discussions, or the experiences shared by others. The four-hour gathering ends with prayers.

Pastors sign a covenant agreeing to take their attendance, prayer, preparation, and follow-through seriously. They also agree to common rules concerning honesty, respect, confidentiality, mutual support, and patience.

More than 90 percent of full-time clergy in the conference have participated in at least one year of PLD. A majority have attended for three years or more. Many move on from PLD groups to Peer Mentoring groups as they commit themselves to a Healthy Church Initiative Consultation, which is described in the next chapter. The planning team created three editions of the curriculum with different readings and topics—*PLD* for the first year, *PLD Two* for the second, and *PLD Next* for the third and following years.

Nine-month cycles follow school calendar years, giving pastors a summer break. After several years of offering PLD, the conference is now exploring ways to refresh the model to reengage pastors with quality peer-learning experiences while preserving the basic elements that make PLD work. Not everyone participates every year, and the conference plans intentional fallow periods of lesser activity. Breaks and pauses give time to renew leaders.

A clergywoman said, "When the conference adopted language related to fruitfulness and accountability, I feared negative effects on our sense of connection. Instead, I've never felt more connected to my colleagues than I do today. We know each other better than ever before, and we support each other. It has made a huge difference."

Peer learning binds people together, breaks isolation, increases trust, enhances leadership and morale, and fosters a common sense of mission. It's an expression of a missional connectionalism.

The Strategy Expands

Pastoral Leadership Development groups provide the foundational tactic for our strategy for clergy peer learning. The program benefits from several other tactics that contribute to a more comprehensive strategy.

Other tactics include:

Common readings and learning times for the cabinet. Several times a year, the cabinet adopts a book (frequently one from the PLD list) to study and discuss together.

Common readings and learning time for the Mission Council. The six annual meetings of the Mission Council include an hour or more of discussion on an assigned reading.

Replacing Ministers' School with Converge. The conference entrusted gifted leaders with designing an annual clergy gathering with high-quality time for worship and learning. In early September, *Converge* launches our PLD, Residency in Ministry, and other peer-learning experiences and welcomes new clergy into our community.

Surge for college-age ministries. Surge has become an annual learning event for everyone holding leadership in college-age ministries, including students, pastors, and campus ministers.

Adopting the PLD model for the Residency in Ministry program. Provisional elders and deacons experience continuous peer learning at the beginning of their ministry.

A PLD module for full-time youth directors. Missouri contracted with a well-known youth leader to facilitate this specialized group.

A conference reading list. The bishop, cabinet, and staff regularly update a reading list of nearly forty books to distribute across various gatherings and teams. Whenever pastors gather, nearly everyone present has read ten or more books from the reading list! This fosters common language and purpose.

Lay Leadership Development groups. The conference lay leader worked with others to develop a parallel nine-month experience for laity that corresponds with PLD, using the same readings and a modified handbook. LLD grew from twenty attendees to more than a hundred participants a year. Local churches adapted the model for training their own laity.

Small Church Initiative and learning events for part-time pastors. As participation expanded for full-time pastors, the conference initiated other learning groups accessible to those who serve part-time.

Annual conference speakers, workshops, and book studies. Conference sessions include multiple learning components, often involving authors of books used in PLD. Free books are distributed related to the theme of conference, paid for by a book fund created when we ended the conference library.

Catalyst events. Several times a year, the conference offers seminars on specific areas of practice or leadership.

Affinity learning events. The conference offers learning events targeting specific affinity groups, such as Hispanic ministries leaders, large church pastors, or church planters.

District and conference learning opportunities. Several districts and congregations offer one-day events or annual institutes.

Pursuing these tactics has fundamentally changed the conversation about the mission and purpose of conference. In years past, district meetings and clergy gatherings focused on the general church, apportionments, the conference staff, the budget, the number of districts, and a host of other internal mechanisms of our structural connectionalism. Now such gatherings almost entirely focus on what people are trying in their congregations, ideas for youth ministry, and leading change in churches. Cultivating a culture of learning has shifted the focus outward toward the mission field.

Roles

In the Missouri Conference, the Director of Pastoral Excellence carries the portfolio for Pastoral Leadership Development groups, Residency in Ministry, Converge, Surge, coaching, and other learning systems for clergy. She collaborates closely with the Director of Congregational Excellence. She is a member of the cabinet, and encourages superintendents to utilize coaches for themselves and to invite pastors into PLD. She has direct access to the bishop.

The bishop models belonging to a peer-learning community through his own participation, leads a peer-learning group, invites writers and speakers to annual conference, and generally promotes the clergy peer-learning strategy.

The lay leader coordinates Lay Leadership Development groups, and regularly teaches laity about the importance of supporting their pastors' participation in learning groups.

Superintendents invite participation by pastors in various events and inquire about educational plans during pastoral evaluations. They encourage pastor-parish relations committees to support their pastor's learning plan by granting time and funding. No church member would go to a dentist or hire a tax consultant who doesn't stay current with their profession, and laypersons shouldn't expect anything less from their pastors.

Pastors drive the success of a continuous peer-learning plan. Their interest in learning, their desire for quality, and their willingness to teach and learn together are the bedrock of any strategy for clergy peer learning. No conference can mandate learning.

Proximate and Ultimate, Measurable and Describable

How can conferences evaluate the success of a strategy? How can we know a program is having the effect we want it to have? Do any of these strategies ultimately help us make disciples of Jesus Christ and transform the world?

A persistent focus on fruitfulness means the conference attends to outcomes, results, and impact even when many aspects of ministry are fundamentally immeasurable and most fruitful results are long-term.

It's helpful to distinguish between proximate outcomes and ultimate outcomes and to recognize that some outcomes are measurable and that many results that can't be quantified are nevertheless describable.

Proximate outcomes are those middle steps that take us toward a goal.[5] No one can build a house without hundreds of middle steps. Identifying a location, purchasing land, signing papers, negotiating a loan, working with an architect, finalizing a design, contracting with a builder—these are only a few of the many proximate outcomes. None of these steps individually results in a new house, but no one can build a house without successfully completing each of them. They are worthwhile, helpful, and necessary lesser goals that lead toward the ultimate outcome.

Jesus commissioned his disciples to reach people with the good news of God's love in Christ in a manner that changes lives and changes the world. Our ultimate vision is nothing less than the coming of God's kingdom on earth.

Increasing the number of vital congregations that make disciples of Jesus Christ for the transformation of the world is an ambitious and worthy goal since faith communities are the most significant arena where disciple making takes place. But what are the proximate outcomes that are necessary for increasing the number of vital congregations?

Enhancing the skills of pastors, sharpening their leadership ability, grounding them in scripture, connecting them to the support of colleagues—accomplishing these does not alone lead to the fulfillment of the mission of

Christ in the world. But it's impossible to imagine strengthening the ministry of our churches and increasing their capacity to reach next generations without pastors adept at learning, growing, and leading. The components of a strategy for clergy peer learning are proximate outcomes, worthy of our best effort and necessary for the long-term fulfillment of our mission.

Chance favors the connected pastor, and consistent with the research described earlier, increasing the numbers of pastors participating in peer learning has corresponded with increased attendance, giving, and mission in our churches.

We can measure the number of pastors who participate and the number of years they attend. As already stated, more than 90 percent of our full-time pastors have participated in PLD during the last four years, and the majority for two or more years. In addition, we can count the number of people who participate in other events, such as Converge, Surge, Lay Leadership Development groups, and district and local church training events. Participation trends indicate interest, relevance, and quality. In most cases, we see rapid or steady increases during the early years of an initiative, and then a tapering off until the event is redesigned or repurposed.

We can also measure how frequently or regularly the cabinet or Mission Council invests in learning time, or what percentage of our time during annual conference sessions goes toward learning rather than receiving reports. Are our trends indicative of a learning culture or a reporting culture?

We can even measure how many days per year superintendents, staff, or the bishop spends in learning events for their own skill enhancement.

And for all these initiatives, we can invite subjective evaluation by the participants. What do pastors find most helpful? What could be done better? What would be most helpful in the future?

A few steps closer to ultimate outcomes, we can measure the trends of our churches. After more than forty years of uninterrupted decline in attendance, the Missouri Conference has increased attendance during five of the last nine years. Giving to mission, apportionment support, numbers of new church starts—these numbers are all increasing. While it's nearly impossible to separate out the variables that lead to these trends, one influence is the increasing number of pastors who are clear about their mission, are confident about the future, are learning new approaches, and feel supported and encouraged in their work.

And yet many aspects of ministry are fundamentally immeasurable. With these immeasurable elements, we describe changes we see and experience.

A pastor's wife pulled me aside at annual conference and said, "What have you people done to my husband?" At first, I couldn't tell whether she was angry or pleased. With tears in her eyes, she said, "I haven't seen him as positive about ministry or as eager to go to work since he was in seminary years ago. He's rediscovered his calling! He's enjoying ministry again, and so am I." She was describing her husband's participation in a PLD group.

With the support one pastor found from coaching and conference staff, she approached her superintendent about an ambitious plan to re-start a declining urban church. Several months later, the pews are buzzing with enthusiastic young people as the plan came to fruition.

Another pastor initiated a conversation in her congregation to start a new church. Another pastor led his congregation to repurpose a building to serve as an alternative worship site for reaching the poor.

There are hundreds of such stories describing the fruit of ministry. Many emerge directly from specific learning experiences. For many more, the relationship is less direct, and a robust focus on peer learning provides only one variable that contributes to the outcome.

Other questions we consider when we think of the unquantifiable fruit of our strategies include the following: Are more pastors seeking account-ability? Is there a more hopeful spirit about the future? Are we asking better questions now than before about our mission field? Are more laity learning about church dynamics? Are more congregations training other congrega-tions? Are topics discussed at charge conferences and district meetings be-coming more relevant to our mission? Is a common language making us more disciplined and focused on the mission? Are there identifiable signs of collaboration that weren't visible before? Are pastors and laity feeling better equipped for ministry? These are all fruitfulness questions.

The overall effect of a strategy for clergy peer learning has been to re-inforce a missional identity better attuned to the context around us, to pro-vide common readings that foster a common language, and to deepen mu-tual accountability. The strategy draws people into the mission of reaching people and changing lives for Jesus Christ.

Specificity and Strategies

A consensus is emerging about what most significantly impacts the mission of a conference. The Seven Levers are an attempt to articulate that consensus as a series of strategies.

Strategies should be specific enough to give direction. Leaders should consider, "Is the strategy one that provokes action? Does it help people know what to work on?"

Conference leaders easily turn to phrases that are too nebulous. Seeking justice, making disciples, and transforming the world—these describe ultimate ends. These may send our hearts soaring, but strategies operate closer to the ground. They suggest how we shall spend our time tomorrow and next week and next year.

Jesus reveals the nature and love of God. That's his purpose. His *strategies* involved such things as teaching in the temple, forming communities of followers, sending disciples out in pairs, telling stories that illustrate God's kingdom, and exemplifying the unexpected love of God by stepping across social boundaries.

A strategy doesn't require a ten-page report. But it does need enough specificity to give direction to everyone who wants to come along. Leaders sometimes puzzle over why people throughout the organization aren't doing more to help. Maybe it's because they receive no clear signals about what's important to work on. That's the value of succinct strategies.

Can you summarize a few strategies of your conference? Would others describe them nearly the same as you?

The key question is, "What might a strategy for clergy peer learning look like for our conference?" and not, "Will we use these particular programs to fulfill the strategy?"

Starting new churches and drawing pastors into peer-learning experiences are the first two levers. And yet the majority of pastors serve churches with long-standing downward trends rather than congregations full of hope and promise. Is there a strategy for revitalizing existing congregations? This takes us to the third lever, a strategy for congregational intervention.

Conversation Questions

Ask your pastor about how he or she learns best. What setting is most effective for deepening understanding, sharpening skills, learning group dynamics, and practicing leadership? How does your congregation support the learning and growth of your pastor?

When have you belonged to a peer-learning group that was helpful, sustaining, and spiritually satisfying? What qualities of the experience made it so? How did it affect your leadership and ministry? What did you learn about yourself? Your work? About Christ? What would cause you to commit to participation in a peer-learning group?

What challenges do you see to making a clergy peer-learning project scalable in your conference and accessible to a large number of clergy?

How important is it for participation to be voluntary? How important is it for the content to focus on practical skills and leadership?

What's the role of conference in cultivating clergy peer learning, and what responsibility rests with pastors to take initiative? How might a quality peer-learning program impact the ministries of your conference?

What are some of the tactics (programs, initiatives, ministries, or resources) that contribute to your conference's strategy for clergy learning? What other organizations or congregations contribute to clergy learning in your area?

What proximate outcomes give you the sense that your conference is making progress on clergy development? How do you deal with the fact that some outcomes are clearly measurable and some are not?

Describe what a strategy for clergy learning might look like in your conference. What would you be willing to do to help develop such a strategy?

The Third Lever

A Strategy for Congregational Intervention

The third lever for conferences is a strategy for intervening to renew congregations and to reengage them with their mission field in order to reverse patterns of decline and aging. The majority of pastors serve congregations with forty years of uninterrupted decline, churches that resist significant change. An intervention system serves as a catalyst for change, challenging churches to face issues they have avoided and offering support for redirecting their mission.

According to the Towers-Watson Report, 15 percent of United Methodist churches fulfill the study's criteria for vital congregations—outward focused, receiving new members, growing in attendance, reaching multiple generations, financially healthy, and actively engaged in community service and world mission. Vital congregations come in all sizes and contexts—small, medium, and large; urban, suburban, and rural. These congregations are clear about their mission and confident about their future.

A similar number of churches are likely on the other end of the spectrum, congregations that are so inward focused, ridden with conflict, resistant to change, or financially strapped that their future seems irreversibly bleak.

Between these extremes are the vast majority of United Methodist congregations, churches that operate well with generally healthy lay and clergy leadership, and yet their average age slowly increases and attendance slowly declines. Finances become more difficult as older members pass away at a faster rate than new members join. Operating budgets increase, staff salaries grow, and facilities require more care with fewer people to share the costs. These congregations provide worship in styles that reach ever-shrinking niches of the population. They are served by pastors and laity who work hard, but see little change. Nothing is noticeably broken, no one feels a sense of crisis, and yet the congregation slowly grows older while the community trends younger, and the church becomes smaller as the population grows larger. If nothing interrupts the trajectory, these issues become more acute until there are no longer the personal and financial resources to reverse directions.

The combined resources—pastors, staff, lay leaders, worship services, ministries, missions, facilities, budgets, and volunteers—of these 70 percent of our congregations comprise the greatest potential missional assets of The United Methodist Church. Together these are the engine that drives our denomination. We can never "church plant" ourselves out of decline. A conference must develop a strategy for increasing the number of existing congregations that are vital—from 15 to 20 to 30 percent or more—and this requires a strategy for congregational intervention. Conferences can't watch and do nothing as historically strong congregations grow old and slowly decline, or they fail in their fundamental mission as conferences.

A Slow Subtle Decline

How do churches that thrive for generations begin to age and decline? A large number of organizational dynamics and societal influences are at work. Churches begin with an outward focus, actively attentive to the community around them, or else they never survive their first few years. They become effective at reaching out, inviting, and assimilating new people into their ministries, or else they fail. As churches mature, more of their energy focuses on internal issues—buildings, budgets, staff, and the needs and preferences of their existing membership. Without intentional effort to focus outward, they unknowingly begin to operate more for the benefit of the insiders than for the community of people around them. Pastors take care of their flocks, and congregations take care of their pastors. Satisfied congregations become complacent, simply repeating last year's ministries again this year with a few minor improvements. They stick with staff configurations that worked thirty years ago and offer worship in styles appreciated by longtime members. Congregations become passive, expecting new people to find them, like them, and join them in their predictable, comfortable patterns. In ways so subtle that no one notices, fewer people join than before and the average age increases by a few years every decade. Extrapolate this pattern for fifty years, and a formerly strong, vibrant congregation slowly weakens.

Every five years or so, congregations need to rethink, repurpose, and renew themselves in order to avoid moving into a stagnant or declining phase of the life cycle. They need to reinvent themselves, recapturing their original sense of purpose while adjusting strategies for the changing contexts around them. They must deeply engage questions such as the following: Who are we? What are we here for? Who is our neighbor? What particular mission has God given us, and what are we going to do about it?

This is not unlike the reinvention other institutions and businesses undergo regularly. Think about how differently banks serve their community now compared to forty years ago. In decades past, community banks worked at one downtown location, offering traditional services, such as checking accounts and loans. Customers came to them, paid for parking, and stood in line. Now no bank could survive without branch locations, online banking, debit cards, mobile phone apps, and other personalized and immediately accessible services. Banks serve the same purpose as forty years ago but with radically different strategies. Decades ago, universities required students to live on campus, attend classes in person, and buy books from the campus store. Now universities have remote learning sites and provide online courses with downloadable textbooks. Cultivating a sense of purpose, rethinking operations, and reengaging the community is difficult but essential work.

Intervention

Usually, churches change slowly and in incremental steps. They identify a particular opportunity or unmet need, build consensus, align resources, and initiate a ministry. Or they mobilize to overcome an obstacle that limits their ministry by a process of studying, learning, planning, gathering support, and making the necessary changes. By such means, churches add a staff member, renovate a building, buy a youth van, or start a new worship service.

Rethinking the overall purpose and operations of a church is a larger task requiring different tools, higher resolve, and more expertise. Some churches successfully undertake such a task on their own using a variety of programs and resources.

However, the task usually benefits from outside consultation. Experienced consultants can see problems that people immersed in the daily operations of the church can't see. They bring greater objectivity to the task of evaluating systems. Outside consultants can say things that insiders could never say and suggest courses of action that many members may intuitively know are necessary but which they could never articulate.

The letters of Paul demonstrate the power of an outside perspective for influencing the health of congregations. Paul intervenes in discussions and conflicts in Corinth, Rome, and Ephesus with ideas and suggestions that remind people of the purpose of the church and direct their energies toward following Christ and reaching outside themselves. He clarifies, challenges, consoles, and confronts the congregations with love and affection. He warns them when they become complacent, are distracted by unnecessary pursuits, or exhibit strife that diminishes the power of their witness. He uses language that helps them understand their purpose. By describing the church as the body of Christ, he unifies them and reminds them that each member of the body is important and that in Christ our ministries complement each other. He describes the work of the Holy Spirit building us into the people of God, with Christ the chief cornerstone. Paul mobilizes churches toward the mission of Christ.

John Wesley and early superintendent ministers provided the same role for Methodist faith communities scattered across Great Britain. Francis Asbury did the same for the churches in America. These leaders preached, taught, corrected, challenged, and encouraged congregations. They were honest to point out the incongruity between the values congregations espoused and the reality of their current operations. They continually fine-tuned the mechanisms for ministry and invited pastors and laity to do the same. They kept the church relevant and engaged, focused and outward leaning, grounded in Christ and moving forward.

The word *intervention* frequently has negative connotations, suggesting interference or uninvited advice or pressure. *Intervention* can sound coercive, heavy-handed, or unwanted, and brings to mind people meddling where they don't belong.

At its most basic, *intervention* means "to come in" from the outside, and effective interventions promote healthy behavior or reshape negative directions. In therapy, an intervention refers to an orchestrated attempt by family and friends to get someone to seek help with an addiction or another serious problem. An intervention points out the discrepancy between someone's stated values and their actual behavior. An intervention opens the doors to healthier options. Interventions provide people a new path to take.

Interventions and outside perspective helps churches break through dynamics that keep them trapped and unable to change. When I was a young pastor, I led our congregation through a series of learning experiences that identified our parking limitations, our need for small-group ministries, better visitor assimilation, and staff realignment. Conversations were vigorous and helpful, but we had trouble taking action. People felt uncomfortable committing to the recommendations that leaders were presenting. Months of conversations resulted in refined plans but no action. At one point, I invited an experienced pastor to meet with the leadership. He repeated the same material we had discussed for months. When he left, everyone turned to me and asked, "Why aren't we doing those things?"—as if nobody had ever heard of these ideas before! We listen differently to outside voices. They confirm truths we already know. They give us permission we can never give ourselves.

Using outside expertise overcomes another dynamic that limits change. When a pastor introduces a new idea, he or she faces predictable questions as the laity mull over the suggestion. Laypersons may simply be doing their due diligence, analyzing alternatives, projecting costs, considering how to proceed. But sometimes it feels like the clergyperson is on one side of a table facing laypersons on the other side in an oppositional posture. Push and push back, tit for tat, back and forth. It feels like clergy and laity are at odds with each other when they are all simply trying to move the mission forward.

When an outside consultant makes a bold recommendation, the dynamics are different. Metaphorically, the consultant sits on one side of the table and the laity and clergy sit *together* on the other side. The pastor and lay leaders have to respond together to the analysis or recommendation. What do we make of this idea? Would that work here? Is that something we really need to do? When the laity and clergy process ideas together, they build a more cohesive team. An outside perspective makes this possible.

While analyzing the downward trajectory of our churches, the leaders of the Missouri Conference began to explore a system for intervention. We wanted a comprehensive experience using outside expertise to help congregations face the hard realities and make the tough choices that would break through denial, avoidance, and blame. We wanted congregations to see before themselves a variety of new paths and feel encouraged and supported to take them. We searched for a strategy for congregational intervention.

Early Experiments

A variety of tools help congregations reconsider their purpose, realign their operations, and reconnect with the mission field. Congregations were already reaching for resources and doing considerable work on their own, using books such as *Holy Conversations* by Gil Rendle and Alice Mann, *Unbinding the Gospel* by Martha Grace Reese, and *The Purpose Driven Church* by Rick Warren. Several churches worked together on an urban academy model. These approaches used written resources to lead the process. Outside expertise came in a book.

As Gil Rendle says, "Every program works—somewhere." In other words, every model proves helpful to some churches and doesn't work with other churches. The first tactic of our strategy is to encourage churches to use the resources listed above. Doing any of these is better than doing nothing!

I wrote *Five Practices of Fruitful Congregations* for churches as they rethink their systems.[1] *Five Practices* offers Radical Hospitality, Passionate Worship, Intentional Faith Development, Risk-Taking Mission and Service, and Extravagant Generosity as the unifying practices to focus a congregation's mission. Abingdon Press worked with me to create a congregation-wide, six-week immersion experience for *Five Practices*. Hundreds of churches used the material for sermon series or small group study. *Five Practices* stimulates congregations to improve their current systems, but seldom fosters comprehensive or disruptive change. For instance, it helps a congregation improve their worship, outreach, and assimilation, but it doesn't address how to realign staff to reach younger generations or how to streamline congregational governance. *Five Practices* created an appetite for more substantial consultation and intervention. Congregations want to change.

A variety of one-time or short-term events served as another tactic. The conference brought in guest speakers, consultants, and pastors to teach on topics such as staffing the large church, safe borrowing for capital funds, improving stewardship, or preaching in the small church. We collaborated with the Missouri United Methodist Foundation, Horizons, Texas Methodist Foundation, the Rueben Job Center, the Lewis Center for Church Leadership, and other seminaries and institutes. Individual congregations contracted with consultants for more in-depth work.

These approaches brought outside perspectives to bear on the internal workings of congregations, and yet we were still merely addressing individual components of church operations. We wanted a comprehensive model for more in-depth engagement, a model that was affordable to most congregations and portable enough to utilize in a variety of settings. The result was the Healthy Church Initiative (HCI).

The Healthy Church Initiative

Six pastors met around a kitchen table to talk about how to strengthen their own ministries and how to help congregations reach out toward their mission fields. They invited Paul Borden, author of *Hit the Bullseye*, to meet with them. He had experimented with an intervention system in his own denomination with some success. The pastors asked Borden to lead an intervention for a Missouri congregation, Church of the Shepherd in St. Charles, so that they could watch and learn. Afterward, Bob Farr, pastor of Church of the Shepherd, led interventions in four other churches. Like a tech start-up in a garage, the Healthy Church Initiative began simply and without outside sponsorship by the conference.

Following these successful pilot projects, conference staff discussed how to integrate some of the critical features gleaned from Borden's work into a comprehensive intervention process, and they worked to "Methodize" some of his key teachings to make them more relevant and appropriate for United Methodist theology, polity, and culture.

We selected the pastors and laity we wanted to train to assure a team of consultants with experience at growing churches and leading change, the ability to discern organizational dynamics, and the capacity to communicate well with people in a forthright way with grace and patience.

As the conversation matured, we realized that the word *intervention* was too heavily laden with negative connotations. People perceived that interventions were for congregations which had serious problems or that exhibited dysfunctional behavior. In fact, we wanted to reach healthy congregations that would benefit from rethinking their mission. And *intervention* sounds too assertive and coercive in contrast to our desire to establish an entirely voluntary process.

We shifted our language from *intervention* to *consultation*. The critical question was how to offer the tools to congregations that help them engage their mission in fresh ways. The result was the Healthy Church Initiative, which has become our principal tactic in our strategy for congregational intervention.

The Healthy Church Initiative has multiple components.

Pastoral Leadership Development groups. First, pastors participate for nine months in a Pastoral Leadership Development group to learn basic leadership and organizational dynamics. At the end of PLD, pastors are asked whether they wish to engage their congregations with a consultation weekend. If they don't feel ready, the pastor may continue in PLD for another year. If they wish to proceed with a consultation, pastors work with their lay leadership to schedule an HCI consultation weekend several months in the future. The conference only offers HCI consultations to congregations who vote to participate.

Peer-mentoring groups. When a pastor and congregation agree to an HCI consultation, the pastor enrolls in a peer-mentoring group rather than continuing in PLD. Similar to PLD, the peer-mentoring group reads assigned books and meets monthly with peers who are also preparing for a consultation with a trained leader. PLD focuses on general leadership skills while peer mentoring focuses on the specific prescriptions that result from the HCI consultation, with attention to leading change, moderating resistance, and accessing support systems for pastors.

Coaching. In addition, pastors participating in peer mentoring are assigned a trained coach. By integrating a coaching component into HCI, the planning team added extraordinary value to the experience for pastors. For some people, coaching refers to expensive, executive-style engagement. Others think of a guide for spiritual formation, or they picture volunteer mentoring from an untrained colleague. The planning team wanted quality coaching with trained people attuned to the unique leadership challenges of pastors.

Coaching doesn't involve telling people what to do, like a football coach calling the plays from the sideline. Instead, coaching provides a trusted confidant who explores our hesitancies from an objective perspective, and gives us courage to follow our intuition or offers caution when we react personally to systemic issues. Coaches hold us accountable to our own aspirations and values. The conference considered establishing a coaching program for any pastor who requested it, but in the end, we integrated coaching into the clergy peer-learning experience for HCI.

The peer-mentoring experience has a personal and confidential component through coaching, and a community and collaborative component through monthly meetings with peers, which include assignments that engage pastors with the thinking of experts. This mix provides a learning environment that prepares pastors to lead their congregations through change.

With these components in place, the congregation forms a prayer team, a vision and leadership team, and an assessment team. These teams have specific responsibilities that prepare the congregation for the HCI consultation weekend. They also gather extensive information about the congregation, its history, statistics, finances, staffing, small groups, mission work, assimilation programs, and facilities.

A weekend date is agreed upon with the consultants. Several weeks before the HCI consultation, a teaching session is held with laity about cultural change, the *Five Practices*, and other resources on church leadership.

Several months before the HCI consultation weekend, a "mystery visitors" program begins with the consent of the pastor and lay leader, similar to "mystery shoppers" evaluations done for businesses. Trained visitors engage the congregation numerous times to evaluate the receptivity of the congregation and to record impressions about the worship services and ministries of the church. Mystery visitors attend worship, phone to inquire about children's ministries, visit adult classes, ask about youth ministries, and even stop at nearby convenience stores to ask directions to the church to see how familiar the congregation is to nonmembers. A mystery visitors' report, recording up to forty or more contacts and stretching to sixty pages, is prepared for use in the consultation.

A team, including a trained consultant, a coach, and at least two laypersons, lead the HCI consultation weekend, which runs from Friday through Sunday. They review the information gathered beforehand by the leadership teams, the mystery visitors' report, and demographic studies of the area. The consultants meet personally with each staff member and pastor. They interview laity holding formal leadership positions as well as other members of the congregation. The consultants lead focus groups that have been organized before their arrival. They hold conversations with leadership teams. On Saturday, they teach sessions about the changing context of ministry, the demographics of the area, the mission and purpose of the church, and organizational dynamics of congregations.

Late Saturday evening, the consultants distill all they have learned, read, seen, and heard into a written report that identifies and describes five strengths of the congregation, five concerns, and five prescriptions for the future. On Sunday, one of the consultants preaches at all the worship services, and then presents the written report, which is called the prescription report.

The prescriptions differ with each congregation, and they vary widely in their complexity and difficulty. One prescription might be to form an ongoing prayer team, while another may involve completely reconfiguring the church's staff, renovating a critical room, starting a new worship service, realigning the budget, changing the governance systems, or ending an unfruitful endeavor. The prescriptions are intentionally interruptive, stimulating considerable conversation and calling for significant action. Issues that might otherwise take years to ripen are put before the congregation for planning and action. Fulfilling the prescriptions takes six to eighteen months, depending upon their complexity.

The congregation has four weeks to consider whether to accept all five of the prescriptions or to reject them. Congregations can't pick and choose; it's all or nothing. During the four weeks, the pastor and lay leadership hold town hall meetings or house gatherings to communicate and receive feedback on the prescriptions. An HCI-trained leader who didn't participate in the consultation weekend is sent to lead a day of prayer and usually preaches at Sunday services sometime after the church conference vote.

After four weeks, the congregation votes up or down on the prescriptions at a church conference using a written ballot. If the congregation accepts the five prescriptions, the HCI congregational coach meets with lay leaders monthly to help them move forward with their prescriptions, the pastor continues with the peer-mentoring group, and the pastor and congregation begin work on the prescriptions. If the congregation chooses not to accept the prescriptions, the congregation ends its participation in HCI.

The Healthy Church Initiative has become the primary tactic for our strategy for congregational intervention. It's comprehensive. It interrupts current operations in a constructive way. It provides direction for work and offers support for the congregation and the pastor as they make hard decisions. Most importantly, HCI turns the congregation outward toward the mission field.

Evaluating the Results

Since 2007, 103 churches have completed a Healthy Church Initiative consultation weekend. Of those, ninety-six accepted their prescriptions and set to work on them. Seven churches chose not to accept their prescriptions. Interestingly, most of those voting down the prescriptions nevertheless worked on them at their own pace. The process identified issues that the congregations felt they could no longer avoid even if they could not bring themselves to formally commit to action.

Approving significant prescriptions can be disruptive, and many congregations report short-term declines in attendance and financial support. However, by eighteen months after their HCI consultation weekends, most congregations have completed their prescriptions and can see the initial fruit of their work.

Of the eighty-eight churches that then completed their prescriptions, thirty-seven have reversed decline and seen growth for the first time in years. Twenty-nine arrested long-term patterns of decline in worship attendance and have maintained stable numbers. Ten churches that were already growing saw their upward trends strengthened. Twelve churches have seen no noticeable impact on worship attendance.

In addition to worship attendance, the majority of congregations have initiated significant new outreach ministries, become more outward focused, and improved youth or young adult ministries and worship services. Congregations report higher levels of participation in small groups, leadership, and giving.

First UMC in Sikeston, Missouri, had seen attendance slowly fall from 380 in 1998 to 310 in 2009 before they participated in an HCI consultation. Their attendance had surpassed 500 in the 1960s. Their prescriptions challenged the church to engage in local missions, change specific ministry structures and worship practices, and address facility needs to make the church more inviting. During the months that followed, they initiated a community-wide mission blitz known as "Hope Epidemic." They redesigned their newest worship service, overhauled their children's program, and made staff changes, eliminating the position of associate pastor and adding a worship coordinator and discipling coordinator. They also remodeled entryways and replaced signage to direct people toward a more visible entry. Success in these generated confidence and clarity, and now the church is taking on a "Hope Center" ministry. Average attendance now tops 590.

Harrisonville UMC, in Harrisonville, Missouri, held its consultation in January 2011. They discovered that for the previous forty years worship attendance had remained steady at two hundred and that the church had started no new small groups. They had remained insulated from the community. The prescriptions included recommendations to change their governance structure, enhance their Sunday morning services, reevaluate facility use, and rethink their processes for visioning and planning. They offered "bridge events" to connect with the community, including an Easter Saturday service in the parking lot, Vacation Bible School in a local park, and a concert in the park ministry. With each event, they became bolder, reached more people, and drew more people into leadership. They renovated the chapel into a prayer room and developed a prayer team to support all new ministries. They now offer a variety of new small group ministries that provide avenues by which people enter into the life of the church.

HCI congregations report a resurgence of energy and interest, sometimes not directly resulting from the prescriptions but from the unifying and energizing effect of accomplishing major tasks as a congregation. Lay leaders and pastors describe churches operating with a new sense of imperative and waking up to a fresh sense of purpose.

Expanding on the Strategy

Twenty or more consultations each year requires a pool of trained consultants, coaches, and peer-mentoring leaders. Costs related to materials, demographic studies, and the mystery visitors program and for compensating coaches, leaders, and consultants require funding from the congregation and from the conference. HCI has proven to be particularly effective with medium-sized and large congregations, but the model is too personnel-intensive to replicate for the nearly six hundred congregations in the Missouri Conference with fewer than sixty people in attendance. Our tactic for these congregations adapts key components of HCI to create the Small Church Initiative.

The Small Church Initiative (SCI) targets churches served mostly by part-time pastors. Churches send their pastor and a number of laity equal to 10 percent of their worship attendance to four one-day training events each year. Small Church Initiative events host a number of churches in a region to learn together, and the participants are taught by pastors and laypersons with small church experience. SCI covers the same topics as HCI but tailors them to the needs of small congregations. Participants learn new ideas for leading worship, starting small groups and youth ministries, and engaging the community. They learn techniques for reaching out to the unchurched through service ministries. SCI has shown better results in some regions than in others, and we still experiment with variations to see what works best.

As another tactic in the strategy for congregational intervention, the conference adapted the HCI consultation to engage college-age ministries. The College-Age Ministries Initiative, or CMI, focuses on campus ministries, their sponsoring congregations or boards, and the students who participate.

What We've Learned

Intervention ripens issues that otherwise would take years for a congregation to address. It intensifies the process of change.

Pastors demonstrate incredible courage when they invite consultants into their church to analyze, evaluate, and prescribe. They feel vulnerable, self-conscious, and sometimes defensive. It's like inviting a therapist into your home to watch how your family eats, works, and plays together. Courage is essential for leading change.

Interventions work best for congregations that are already healthy. HCI doesn't help churches mired in significant conflict; in fact, it can exacerbate problems.

It takes time to see results. Like the biblical truth suggested in images of seedtime and harvest, sowing and soils, vines and branches, leading congregations to more fruitful ministry involves patience and hope.

Disruptive intervention pushes a congregation into the wilderness of uncertainty and anxiety. When congregations stay the course, they emerge stronger, more focused, and healthier.

Maintaining quality is imperative. Congregations must trust the competence and motivations of consultants, coaches, and everyone involved from the outside. Consultants absorb a great deal of pain, loss, grief, and anger. They must do so without reacting or feeling drawn into personal issues.

HCI is expensive and personnel intensive, and yet every cost-benefit analysis supports continuing and expanding the program. Strengthening long-standing congregations that have been declining changes the morale of the conference.

For special situations, including extraordinarily large churches, some African American congregations, or church starts reaching a new stage, the conference does better to pay for specialized consultants, even if it means inviting people from outside the conference. Gifted, trained laity add extraordinary value when they serve as consultants.

Participation must be voluntary. Remember the old joke, "How many psychologists does it take to change a light bulb? One, but the light bulb has to *want* to change!" Both the pastor and the laity have to want HCI for it to work.

Most congregations yearn to interrupt decline and to reach more people. They want to be stronger ten years from now than they are today. Leaders know things must change, but they need permission to act and the courage to do so.

Who Does What

This lever, a strategy for congregational intervention with HCI as the central tactic, requires the greatest operational collaboration of all the levers. Everyone has a role, and coordination and communication are critical.

The Director of Congregational Excellence carries the portfolio for the Healthy Church Initiative and works as chief consultant, working with an HCI executive committee comprised of his executive assistant and a mix of consultants, pastors, and laity. He invites churches to participate, determines which churches to accept, sets the dates for weekend consultations, and assigns consultants to churches. He also oversees the mystery visitors program, contracting with the company that provides them. A part-time layperson coordinates the Small Church Initiative under the supervision of the director.

The Director of Pastoral Excellence supervises the training and assignment of coaches, and works with the Director of Congregational Excellence to establish the peer-mentoring groups and to train group leaders. She also leads the College-Age Ministries Initiative. The two directors work together on catalyst events and other training experiences.

As bishop, I interpret, promote, and encourage, and I buffer the criticism that interventions elicit. Because of my personal experience as a pastor, I lead a peer-mentoring group for large church pastors.

The role of superintendents and the bishop is important but nuanced. Superintendents promote HCI and identify churches that would benefit from consultations, but they don't participate directly. The presence of a supervisor in the actual interviews and assessment can have a restraining effect on honest conversation. Superintendents attend PLD sessions and weekend training. They offer prayer and encouragement, and they preside over the church conference that votes on the prescriptions. Superintendents that train as consultants work in that role in churches outside their district.

Both the current and previous conference lay leaders are trained as consultants and serve on consulting teams. They are encouraged to do so because of their particular ability to understand and communicate the dynamics of church leadership and not because of the office they hold.

The Director of Connectional Ministries forms the teams that lead the Day of Prayer following an HCI consultation and usually preaches at Sunday services. The Director of Financial and Administrative Ministries serves as a consultant because of his analytical and communication skills and his history of effective pastoral leadership. The Director of Mission, Service, and Justice Ministries leads follow-up training when congregations receive a prescription calling for more robust outreach ministries.

What are the components of your conference's strategy for reversing decline? What tactics make a positive difference? What form might a strategy for congregational intervention take in your conference?

The churches and pastors involved with the Healthy Church Initiative and the Small Church Initiative form a network of mutual support based on their common experience and their passionate desire to focus the church's attention outward toward the mission field. As itineracy deploys clergy to new positions, the pool of pastors who have learned leadership through HCI widens. Some pastors request to serve a church that has completed HCI, and some churches place a premium on receiving pastors with HCI experience.

As with all the Seven Levers, developing an effective strategy for congregational intervention leads to multiple results. When our historically strong congregations become more confident and outward focused, they feel called to start new congregations or to initiate ministries that serve the poor or that reach across the globe. They become streams for future pastoral leadership. It's impossible to imagine how a conference can reverse decline without a significant number of existing congregations rethinking their mission and practice.

Starting new congregations, clergy peer learning, and congregational intervention—these three levers address congregations and the learning habits of current clergy. All three of these require creating new systems within a large, complex organization where authority is distributed diffusely. Even with attention to these, a conference can't fulfill its mission without deliberate attention to the quality of clergy leadership. The fourth lever addresses a strategy for cultivating clergy excellence.

Conversation Questions

How does your congregation receive honest, objective, outside appraisal of its ministries? If your church has experienced a slow decline, how do you account for why this has happened?

When was the last time your congregation seriously and thoroughly reexamined its purpose, mission, and operations? What resources were helpful? What did you learn? When are you likely to do such a reappraisal again?

If your church has turned around, refocused its mission, or reconnected to the community in a powerful new way, what was the catalyst that God used? What new ministries emerged? If your church has not experienced such a change, what do you think it will take?

What intervention models have you seen work to reinvigorate congregations? What caused them to work effectively? Which would you be willing to try?

What role or responsibility do you think the conference holds for addressing the decline of congregations?

How do you suppose your congregation would respond to an intervention? What anxieties or questions would have to be addressed? What would cause them to invite such thorough analysis, teaching, and recommendations from outside voices?

How is courage an essential quality for leading change?

If your congregation hosted an intervention weekend, what prescriptions do you suppose the consultants might offer? Why might these recommendations have a greater impact than similar recommendations made by current leaders of the congregation?

The Fourth Lever

A STRATEGY FOR CULTIVATING CLERGY EXCELLENCE

The fourth lever is a strategy for cultivating clergy excellence, and this involves changing the fundamental values that drive clergy recruitment, credentialing, evaluation, and deployment to focus on fruitfulness and excellence.

The previous levers develop systems for starting new congregations, clergy peer learning, and congregational intervention. Those three levers are left unaddressed by the *Book of Discipline*, which neither requires nor recommends such strategies and doesn't restrain conferences from creating processes consistent with their missional needs. Conferences are free to develop, adapt, or organize their work to address those strategies any way they please.

The fourth strategy, however, requires working within the requirements of the *Discipline* that are beyond the capacity for any conference to change. This chapter isn't about changing the *Discipline*'s processes or working around them. Rather, it focuses on how to infuse the entire clergy development system with higher expectations, better communication, greater consistency, and support for candidates and pastors in their professional and personal development. A conference can follow the letter and the spirit of the *Discipline* while also introducing a higher premium on fruitfulness and by directing more attention to the mission field.

Identifying gifted candidates, screening ineffective pastors, and developing a culture of learning and growth—these are the challenges of this strategy. No conference can successfully fulfill its mission without pastors who are capable and equipped to lead congregations effectively.

Multiple Components

Think of all the distinct components that influence the stream of clergy leadership. A strategy for cultivating clergy excellence begins with an inventory of systems that shape clergy from the earliest discerning of God's call through postretirement service and care.

Some of the components include:

Recruitment. How does the conference help people determine whether God is calling them to full-time Christian service? This is the work of congregations, pastors and laity, camping and retreat ministries, campus ministries, and events to explore ministry careers.

Candidacy. This phase involves superintendents, registration with the General Board of Higher Education and Ministry, charge conferences, mentors, reading materials, written work, psychological evaluations, background checks, and interviews with district committees.

Education. Paths include seminary, Course of Study, and conference training programs with related costs, curricula, teachers, and facilities.

Provisional Years. Conferences offer Residency in Ministry, mentors, coaches, or some other form of practicum and supervision.

Credentialing and Ordination. This component involves interviews, evaluations, recommendations, and approval by various committees and the clergy session.

Deployment and Appointment. Cabinets operate with a set of principles and practices that may be explicit and widely known or implicit and unidentified.

Support with Transitions. Conferences assist clergy and their families to begin new appointments successfully and guide congregations on how to send and receive pastors.

Supervision, Accountability, and Evaluation. This includes evaluations, supervision, and the pastor's relationship to the pastor-parish relations committee and superintendent.

Continuing Education, Peer Learning, and Professional Development. These draw pastors into patterns of lifelong learning and mutual accountability.

Salary, Housing, Pensions, Insurance, and Support Systems. Conferences provide benefits to assure the security and health of pastors.

Intervention Systems. These processes respond to misconduct or ineffectiveness.

Retirement and Postretirement Service. In many conferences, the majority of clergy members are retirees. How are they connected, cared for, and offered opportunities to serve?

Toward Greater Consistency

Conferences often address these many components inconsistently. A conference may do well at recruiting future pastors through campus ministries and yet have a candidacy process that intimidates and discourages engagement. As one system opens the door, another system closes it. In one district, candidacy mentors are carefully selected, highly trained, and offered consistent support while in another district, mentoring is unfocused and haphazard. Some Boards of Ordained Ministry work collaboratively with the cabinet while others remain distant, disconnected, or even uncongenial.

The inconsistent quality of our systems provides reason enough to search for a more comprehensive strategy. Every conference has room for improvement.

The Missouri Conference identified several critical issues related to clergy development. For instance, we found ourselves initiating supervisory conversations to remove ineffective pastors who had been ordained during the previous three years. The conference invested years credentialing these pastors and then immediately began a lengthy process to remove them. Something wasn't working.

Also, candidates expressed frustration with inconsistent evaluation. Poor communication between district committees, superintendents, and the board meant candidates received mixed signals about their status or what was expected of them.

The inherent complexity of the credentialing processes seemed irrelevant and impenetrable to many candidates, discouraging them before they even started.

And too many pastors completed all the processes but then proved to be ill equipped for leading congregations, causing discouragement for the pastors, frustration for the churches, and fostering decline in witness. The system didn't provide a reliable stream of people to lead congregations.

Furthermore, the conference focused heavily on elders and deacons while the use of lay ministers and local pastors increases each year. The

Discipline assigns responsibility for credentialing these people to the districts, and this means the greatest number of people are credentialed by the system at its most diffuse, inconsistent, and uncoordinated point.

According to the Lewis Center for Church Leadership, the Missouri Conference deploys 120 fewer elders in pastoral roles today than we did ten years ago, while we appoint 81 more local pastors and lay ministers.[1] Full-time pastoral positions have fallen from 570 to 403 in the same period. Establishing streams of gifted part-time, bivocational, or lay ministers demands attention.

Since the *Discipline* distributes responsibility for clergy systems diffusely, a strategy for cultivating clergy excellence requires looking at each component to see how to improve it. The components can become more coherent and mission focused with a more comprehensive strategy.

What Kind of Leadership?

Contrast the qualities of clergy leadership needed by the church in this era with those valued a few decades ago. Fifty years ago, American culture supported church participation, and during the decades of expansion and prosperity following World War II, the church valued pastors who were dependable, stable, and competent to maintain the institution and to help churches grow incrementally. Pastors stepped into well-defined roles with common expectations. Pastors met the needs of the members already there through personal pastoral care, counseling, and good administration of the church, including qualities we now associate with management. Most pastors adopted a passive approach, waiting for good Christian people to move into their neighborhoods, find their church, and join them in worship. Churches were monocultural, with people of all ages sharing similar tastes in music and in approaches to spirituality.

As Gil Rendle says, "I was trained not to change peoples' lives but to change their [membership] affiliations."[2] This matches my experience. During my early years of ministry, I was taught how to do follow-up visits with those who visited our church and to invite people to transfer their memberships. We assumed people were already Christian and belonged to another church. My approach toward ministry changed when we discovered many people had no church affiliation, and that the people in the community around us had no church experience. We took a more invitational posture and adapted our ministries to reach the unchurched. The gifts needed for managing a passive system in a predominantly religious culture differ significantly from those needed to reach people who have no church background and who view organized religion with suspicion or animosity.

The mission of Christ in the future requires leadership that is more outward focused, risk taking, and able to engage the community. The church needs pastors with an expansive view of the world, multicultural experience, and a willingness to move out of their comfort zones to reach people. We need pastors able to adapt ministry styles to an ever-changing environment, able to lead worship that connects with people with varying ways of approaching God. Pastoral leadership requires resilience, agility, and the capacity to mobilize people toward the mission of Christ.

What kind of pastoral leadership will be needed to fulfill the mission of The United Methodist Church in the future? And how do we identify and cultivate pastors with those qualities and prepare them for different sizes and types of congregations and for an ever-changing mission field? These questions are foundational for a strategy for clergy excellence.

Lovett Weems suggests that leaders ask why we do what we are doing with every component of our clergy systems and that we respond with an answer that begins "So that . . ." Then we ask why we want that outcome, and answer with yet another "So that . . ." until we tie any proposed activity to Christ's mission through the church.[3]

For instance, why do we have a candidacy process, or any of the interviews that comprise it? *So that* we can help people discern and articulate their inner call and *so that* the church can evaluate the gifts that comprise the outward call. Why? *So that* we assure that the people pursuing the role of pastor will serve the church well and bear fruit and protect the church from harm. Why? *So that* our congregations will thrive and more people will experience God's love and feel called to do God's work. Why? *So that* the ministries of our church do the work that Christ does, relieve suffering, serve the poor, and change lives. Why? *So that* we participate in God's plan for ushering in God's kingdom on earth.

To begin with the end in mind changes even the earliest steps. The candidacy process is not merely about completing forms, checking off lists, or meeting the requirements of the *Discipline*. When we begin with the end in mind, we consider what questions, relationships, or experiences most help us identify and prepare someone to usher in God's kingdom in an urban neighborhood teeming with young people or in a rural community inhabited by long-timers.

Common Principles

Christ-Centered, Fruitfulness, Excellence, Accountability, and Collaboration—embedding these five expectations into every component of our clergy systems marks the beginning of a more comprehensive strategy for our particular conference. Every committee and board discusses what these mean for its work.

Our Wesleyan roots also guide us. John Wesley repeatedly outlined his high expectations for pastors. Early examinations for pastors included three elements. First, Wesley considered the candidate's heart: Have they the grace for ministry? Do they know God as a pardoning God? Have they the love of God abiding in them? Do they desire and seek nothing but God? These questions address the spiritual life of pastors and their relationship to Christ. These questions don't probe whether candidates are good leaders of people but whether they are followers of Christ. Do they know God?

Second, Wesley addresses the gifts for ministry. Have they the gifts as well as the grace for the work? This refers to their natural abilities and acquired talents. Are they able to work with people, to teach and preach and lead effectively?

Finally, Wesley inquires about whether people have demonstrated success, or later called fruit, in their ministry. Have they convinced or affected anyone, such that they have received the forgiveness of God and a clear and lasting understanding of the love of God? Is the person an instrument of God's convincing, justifying, and sanctifying grace?[4]

Spiritually grounded, gifted for ministry, and fruitful in their work—these are the Wesleyan standards which, interwoven with the five expectations, give us the foundational values for our clergy systems.

Obviously, the first tactic is to improve every distinct component of the clergy system. Those who administer the systems must never miss an opportunity to select excellent leadership to serve at every level of the process and to work toward continuous improvement. Practice excellence in each component and expect excellence from each candidate. Every event for candidates, training for mentors, interview process, and board meeting should reflect intentionality and excellence.

A second tactic involves repeating and deepening the focus on fruitfulness. Change the questions so as to evaluate fruitfulness—for candidates, provisional members, pastors, superintendents, conference staff, and the bishop. Fruitfulness shapes interviews, evaluations, and appointments.

A third tactic for an effective strategy is to foster communication between district committees, the Board of Ordained Ministry, conference staff, registrars, and the cabinet. Does each know what the others are doing, and do they coordinate on calendars and expectations? Is everyone, including the candidates themselves, aware of the current status of each person and what is expected next?

A fourth tactic involves attending to the experience of the candidates and pastors who are affected by clergy systems. Are processes user-friendly, supportive, and clear? Do people inquiring for information receive responses within twenty-four hours? Are candidates, interviewees, and pastors treated with respect and dignity, even when evaluations or recommendations are negative? Are processes consistent, inviting, encouraging, transparent, and honest?

A fifth tactic is to encourage innovation. Can we explore other approaches, learn from other conferences, or try different models?

Aligning Systems and Clarifying Expectations

Changing practices changes a culture. Addressing enough technical challenges eventually results in adaptive change. The statements in italics below represent our aspirations, followed by small steps we are taking to reform clergy systems. We still wrestle with many of the same issues as before, but we pivot a little more toward where we want to go each time we address an element of the clergy system. Shifting the direction of each component a few degrees toward common outcomes makes a significant difference for the whole conference.

Instead of a passive system that waits for people to discover their call on their own, we shift toward active recruitment to identify, invite, and encourage people to consider full-time Christian service.

For instance, the Hannah Project (named for the biblical figure who offered her child to God's service) guides congregations on how to cultivate the call to ministry.

The conference sends young candidates to the national Exploration event, and on alternating years, the conference offers its own Exploration weekend for people of all ages.

Several congregations have adopted MAC Track (Ministry as Career), the plan used by the Church of the Resurrection to prepare young people for ministry.

All major conference youth gatherings include invitations for those discerning their call. The bishop invites anyone considering ministry to come forward at the close of each ordination service.

Youth programs and college-age ministries are the most common streams for providing future pastors. The conference encourages internships for college students. Just as no one should enroll in medical school who has never seen how clinics operate, no one should leave for seminary without experiencing work through a congregation.

Instead of a default of "If you complete all the requirements and have done nothing egregious, you will be approved," we shift to the default of "You may expect not to be approved unless you exhibit outstanding gifts and identifiable fruit for ministry."

Interviews with candidates frequently focus on high-point experiences of the person's spiritual journey or on their personal passions. They talk about mission projects that changed their lives, worship services that drew them toward God, or retreats that awakened them to Christ. These are important aspects of the call. However, if the conference eventually licenses or ordains candidates, those persons never again merely work on a mission project, attend a worship service, or participate in a retreat. Instead, they will be expected to lead teams, plan worship, and teach at retreats. Fruitful ministry mobilizes people. "When was a time you started a Bible class, and how did it go? When did you lead a mission team, and what did you learn? When have you started a new worship service?" These questions explore fruitfulness.

Too often, interviews focus on the candidates' passions. "I have a heart for the poor . . ." Or "I have a passion for young people . . ." A focus on fruitfulness would press further. "How are you currently working with the poor or with young people? How have these passions formed critical decisions in your life, such as where you live, work, or volunteer? What are you actually doing now that expresses this calling and affects lives?" Licensing and ordination don't permit or authorize someone to serve; they confirm someone's pattern of service and their call to leading and multiplying ministry for the sake of Christ.

Other branches of our Wesleyan family are less timid about fruitfulness. In the Methodist church in Vietnam, candidates who express interest in ministry must first start at least three cell groups and then organize the cells into a house church. After this, they begin their interviews and they take their first steps toward licensing or ordination. Cuban Methodism operates in a similar fashion. The experiences of fruitful ministry are evaluated and evidenced before a call is validated by the church.

This shift reshapes candidacy, refocuses mentoring, raises expectations for credentialing, and gives guidance to lifelong evaluation. Merely meeting basic requirements and avoiding egregious behavior isn't enough.

Instead of blaming seminaries for not providing practical education, we shift toward the conference taking responsibility for teaching the basic practices of ministry.

Through internships, Residency in Ministry, coaching, and Pastoral Leadership Development groups, the conference offers formative support in the practice of ministry.

Instead of a candidacy process that bounces those inquiring from person to person with unclear or confusing answers, we shift toward consistency.

Like several other conferences, Missouri offers a Candidacy Summit that brings candidates from all districts together for a weekend of inspiration, learning, and discernment. Candidates get their questions answered, review the steps toward ministry, and can complete their profiles, background checks, and psychological exams in one setting.

Instead of high expectations only for entering candidates, we shift toward evaluating for excellence and fruitfulness throughout ministry.

Pastors annually complete a self-evaluation and the pastor-parish relations committee completes an evaluation. These serve as a foundation for the district superintendent's face-to-face evaluation for each pastor. All evaluations focus on fruitfulness, learning, and next steps and align with the five practices and five expectations that the conference has identified as essential. Evaluations are distinct from consultations about appointments so that the focus remains on support, learning, and growth for ministry.

All superintendents and conference directors also undergo evaluations. These evaluations, along with that of the bishop, involve feedback from dozens of pastors and laity.

Instead of an appointment process shrouded in secrecy and driven by tenure, age, social promotion, personal acquaintance with the district superintendent, or the "good old boy network," we shift toward a system grounded in fruitfulness, affinity to the mission field, and potential.

The cabinet prepares for appointments by compiling attendance and ministry patterns for each church and pastor, reviewing evaluations and consultation forms, studying the demographics of the mission field, and focusing on the mission of the church and the fruitfulness of the pastor.

The cabinet annually refines the principles for appointments before beginning the discernment process. They identify critical appointments, not based on size, salary, or prestige but on potential for impacting the mission field.

The bishop and cabinet explore options, consult with pastors and congregations, and take time to research, reflect, and discern before making appointments. Attention is given to transitions. The cabinet follows detailed protocols to offer appointments, to introduce pastors to congregations, to announce appointments, and to support pastors with transition workshops.

Criteria for selecting superintendents parallel those for assigning pastors. Superintendents and conference directors must have demonstrated fruitful ministry.

The bishop works to make the appointment system as transparent as possible. The bishop walks through each step of the appointment process in workshops at annual conference and clergy events, and he discusses the principles that guide decisions. New appointments are announced and publicly posted as soon as possible after pastors are introduced.

Instead of ignoring or discouraging alternative expressions of ministry, we shift toward engaging people serving full-time Christian service.

Many talented people serve full-time staff positions in larger congregations as youth directors, worship leaders, musicians, or ministry assistants. An increasing number feel called to ministry, and they even complete seminary, but they have no interest in licensing or ordination. Many are young adults who view conference membership as limiting and the appointment system as unsuitable for them.

Large congregations provide one of the richest streams for future pastoral leadership, and conferences can't afford to ignore the trends. We engage and support alternative expressions of ministry, and we encourage online course work for seminary or revamp Course of Study to accommodate the educational needs specific to their service.

Instead of allowing a pastor's ineffectiveness to impact numerous congregations, we shift toward early intervention with an explicit exiting policy.

The *Discipline* outlines the supervisory process for addressing clergy ineffectiveness, including the possibility of involuntary removal when other remedies don't work and with due process and recommendation by the Board of Ordained Ministry to the clergy session. The convoluted, multipage description in the *Discipline* involves many steps, with superintendents, the cabinet, the bishop, the executive committee, and the Board of Ordained Ministry all playing a role. The *Discipline* describes chargeable offenses that constitute misconduct, but it fails to define ineffectiveness with any specificity.

Many conferences have adopted some form of intervention policy that defines ineffectiveness, outlines steps to engage a person who exhibits ineffectiveness, establishes expectations and timelines for changing behaviors, and documents progress, all the while adhering to both the letter and spirit of the *Discipline* and due process. Our use of such a policy, while rare, has resulted in the improvement of the pastors' performance enough to continue in ministry in about 50 percent of cases, and the eventual withdrawal or retirement of the clergyperson in all other instances.

Instead of the Board of Ordained Ministry, the cabinet, the mentors, and the many district committees operating independently to develop criteria, we shift toward more consistent values and expectations.

The Board of Ordained Ministry and the cabinet meet together once a year for a common learning experience and conversation.

The Board of Ordained Ministry Executive Committee and cabinet read the same resources related to supervision, interviewing, and evaluation.

The board and cabinet work together on an exiting policy that improves pastoral performance, assures due process, and addresses ineffectiveness.

The board chairperson invites the bishop to address the board, not about specific personnel issues but about priorities, trends, supply, and the needs of the churches.

The board chairperson and bishop have direct access to each other and regularly talk through processes and interpretations of the *Discipline*.

The cabinet and board's executive committee meet together to work on common policies, coordinate calendars, and research future trends.

Instead of the metaphor of a pipeline for describing credentialing and ordination processes, we shift to the image of an ecosystem.[5]

Pipeline connotes a linear one-size-fits-all system in which candidates enter on one end and are pushed through for years until they emerge at the other end as deacons, elders, or local pastors. The pipeline metaphor focuses our attention on steps, charts, lists, and successfully checking off all the *Discipline*'s requirements.

Ecosystem draws our attention to the environment that surrounds all candidates and pastors throughout their ministry. Are our habitats conducive to health, growth, and sustainability? Do seeds receive enough moisture and proper soil to grow into saplings, and are the conditions of light and nourishment right to grow into trees and multiply into forests? What threatens to stifle growth or poison processes? A healthy ecosystem fosters diversity and adaptation to the changing conditions surrounding it. In an ecosystem model, growth never ends and everything is interactive—congregations, pastors, boards, cabinets, and processes all contribute to the health of the system. The environment feeds the call to ministry lifelong. Developing clergy excellence is more like growing a garden for the long term than like producing pastors on demand.

List the things you do to repair a leaking faucet. The tools and steps comprise a mechanical process in which the problem and solution are both easily known. Apply the right solution and you can't fail. When you finish, you have returned the faucet to its original condition. You've fixed a problem, but you have not created anything new.

Now list the things you do to grow a tomato. You can do all things right and still fail. You can kill a plant, but you can't make one grow. You can only provide the optimum conditions to increase the likelihood of health and fruitfulness. It's a cultivation process. That's how the clergy ecosystem works.

Instead of . . , a shift toward . . . These words capture the strategy for cultivating clergy excellence. The strategy is about directional change. The conference still wrestles with inconsistent processes, the approval of people who aren't effective in ministry, and systems that are not user-friendly, but we're slowly making progress. Instead of constructing a new ship, something only the *Discipline* and General Conference can do, conferences must determine which direction to go with the ship they have and which compass headings to use.

Infusing the process with the language of excellence and fruitfulness raised fears about other important values, such as clergy morale, diversity, or gender equality, and elicited the critique that "It's only about the numbers." Would raising expectations hurt recruitment?

After nine years of shifting toward fruitfulness and excellence, the Missouri Conference has dramatically increased the number of clergywomen serving large congregations (churches with over four hundred in worship attendance) and starting new congregations. The number of women serving on the cabinet has ranged from four to seven of fifteen members. Clergywomen and men continue in ministry or leave ministry after five years at the same rate. The number of African American pastors has increased, including elders, as has the number of African American members. The number of Hispanic and Asian American pastors has increased. The number of cross-cultural appointments has doubled. The average age of large church pastors in Missouri is among the lowest in the country. A more data-driven focus on fruitfulness has opened opportunities rather than limiting them. This is not to suggest that all pastors receive the appointments they think they deserve, but a focus on fruitfulness opens more doors than an "It's all about who you know" approach or the "good old boy" network ever could.

Morale increases when a conference clarifies expectations and makes processes more consistent. High-performing pastors are given greater responsibility and entrusted with more opportunity. They are set free and invited to take more initiative. Pastors who function at a more moderate level are provided means to enhance skills, learn, grow, and improve. Low performers receive clear expectations, benchmarks, timelines, and consequences. As much as possible, everyone knows where he or she stands. The greatest threat to morale is erratic, unknown, unarticulated, or ill-defined values and inconsistent processes.

Clergy Excellence Belongs to Everyone

In the Missouri Conference, the Director of Pastoral Excellence carries the portfolio for the Hannah Project, Exploration events, the Candidacy Summit, Residency in Ministry, coaching, and Pastoral Leadership Development groups. She evaluates college-age ministries, relates to conference youth ministries, and oversees scholarships and internships funded by the Missouri United Methodist Foundation. She serves on the cabinet and is a member of the Board of Ordained Ministry. She has direct access to the bishop.

The bishop and cabinet repeat, interpret, and deepen the focus on fruitfulness. They regularly reevaluate appointment processes to improve communication and to optimize consultation and discernment.

The Board of Ordained Ministry fulfills the *Discipline*'s mandates while collaborating with the cabinet and district committees to assure greater focus and consistency.

Lay members serve a significant role on district committees and the Board of Ordained Ministry. We ask laity to expect excellence, cultivate excellence, and demand excellence in clergy leadership.

Pastors and congregations identify candidates for ministry. All clergy begin as laypersons, and a bishop can't send anyone to a congregation who was not first sent to the bishop from a congregation. Future pastors are formed by congregations.

Imagine

The fourth lever, cultivating clergy excellence, is foundational to other changes in conference culture. Increasing the number of pastors who are spiritually grounded, gifted for ministry, and fruitful in their work extends the United Methodist witness in every way—stronger congregations, healthier church starts, outward-focused mission—reaching next generations and initiating ministries that change lives and transform the world.

Clergy excellence changes a conference.

Imagine entry processes that are elegant in their simplicity, that embed people in the immediate practice of ministry while deepening theological and historical reflection upon the faith.

Imagine systems tailored to a new generation, relevant to the changing populations we are called to serve, and effective in identifying and cultivating excellence, fruitfulness, and the spiritual capacity to mobilize people in Christ's work.

Imagine systems that foster creativity, experimentation, and exploration and recapture the sense of adventure in ministry.

Imagine congregations cultivating the call among people of all ages.

Imagine conference leaders looking fifteen years into the future, honestly appraising leadership needs for current congregations, focusing on communities that have not been reached or that can't be reached by current churches, and considering what qualities and preparation most help us to fulfill the mission.

Imagine cultivating leadership for the church of the future—reaching people outside the faith, engaging alternative communities, and using unconventional means and unexpected settings for mission.

Imagine inviting, preparing, and equipping a healthy mix of part-time, full-time, bivocational, lay, licensed, and ordained pastors that fit the mission field of the future.

Imagine an itinerate culture of pastors willingly adapting themselves to the mission field by moving from one place and context for ministry to another. And imagine this coexisting with another nonitinerate track for ministry for those serving in specialized settings as needed.

Imagine a Board of Ordained Ministry operating more like a search committee, defining the qualities of pastoral leadership they need, asking for referrals, searching nationwide, inviting interviews, and setting standards rather than passively waiting for who shows up to get their stamp of approval.

Imagine systems that cultivate clergy excellence.

Conversation Questions

When was a time God used your congregation to call someone to full-time Christian service? What ministries influenced the person's call? How have you invited someone with the gifts for ministry to consider God's call?

How does your conference invite gifted young people to consider the call to ministry through mission teams, youth ministries, or camping? Is there an organized strategy for doing so? Who takes responsibility for seeing that the invitation is offered consistently and offered well?

How are your conference's candidacy processes, interviews, and credentialing processes experienced by those exploring or responding to a call to ministry? What does your conference do to make the process more understandable?

What values and expectations drive the credentialing processes for those entering ministry in your conference? How do these same expectations shape clergy, staff, and episcopal evaluations? What could be done to make clergy processes more consistent and transparent?

How do clergy and laity learn about the appointment processes and the values that drive them in your conference?

What role does fruitfulness play for clergy credentialing, evaluation, and deployment?

The chapter includes an exercise that uses "instead of . . . we shift toward . . ." Using this language, describe changes you hope might take place in your conference.

What's the one activity you, your colleagues, or your conference could do, which, if done with excellence and consistency, would have the greatest impact on cultivating clergy excellence?

The Fifth Lever

A STRATEGY FOR ALIGNING BUDGETS AND RESOURCES

Ken Callahan, in his early book on church administration, *Twelve Keys to an Effective Church*, distinguishes key leadership practices that contribute to a sense of satisfaction and meaning—such as worship, small-group learning, mission, and service—from those strategies that merely reduce sources of dissatisfaction—such as providing enough parking, clear signage, sufficient meeting space, and financial issues.[1]

Leaders can pour all their energy into reducing the sources of dissatisfaction, and discover they've made no progress in growing a church because these don't directly impact the mission. On the other hand, leaders who focus entirely on purposeful work without addressing the sources of dissatisfaction and conflict will continually find their work derailed.

The same is true with the Seven Levers. The first four strategies move a conference toward its mission. However, through improving governance and aligning finances, a conference can reduce frustration, criticism, mistrust, conflict, and discontent. These changes thus set the stage for the levers that really change a conference.

No area fosters more acute conflict than finances, apportionments, budgeting, and spending. As happens in many families, conflicts over competing interests, diverse values, fairness, and control, which have nothing to do with finances, can nevertheless erupt on the money battlefield. People read into every change in a budget a host of meanings, including many that were never intended.

A strategy for aligning resources toward the mission is essential if the conference is to chart a new course. Without aligning budgets, planning is empty talk.

Sources of Dissatisfaction

During my first few years as bishop, nearly all issues that sparked conflict, eroded trust, intensified criticism, and distracted from our mission were financial. What follows is a list of concerns that were heard repeatedly from pastors and laity from across the conference. Whether the recommendations from Pathways were going to address them or not provided a critical test for how serious we were about change.

Apportionments are too high. Some small churches were giving 35 percent of their budgets to apportionments, crippling local ministry. Large churches were paying hundreds of thousands of dollars, restraining them from hiring staff.

Apportionments increase every year. While the number of churches and members declined, the conference budget crept up by a couple of percentage points annually.

The apportionment formula is confusing. Growing churches, declining churches, new churches, downtown churches, large churches, and rural churches—each category felt unfairly treated and targeted by the formula. The complexity of the formula made it difficult to understand, and churches could not anticipate future costs accurately.

Campus ministries are ineffective and unfruitful. The conference funded thirteen campus ministries with over $900,000. By their own self-assessments, these ministries reached fewer than 350 students. Pastors demanded that something be done.

People are weary of fighting over funding the college. Each year, the conference debated funding the one college in Missouri with United Methodist roots, Central Methodist University. An otherwise positive relationship between the conference and university was dominated by money issues.

There are too many goals and special offerings. Support for twenty-eight service agencies was apportioned as goals and included in the budget. Pastors were unsure whether goals had the same weight as apportionments, and churches were unclear about what the various agencies did.

Supervisors talk about making disciples, but they evaluate on apportionment payment. A church that increased or decreased its giving received greater praise or censor than it did for its patterns of growth or service.

People worry about future sustainability. Growing budgets were supported by fewer people, raising the average cost per member. If you project membership declines and cost increases, most congregations face an inevitable point of nonsustainability.

The budgeting process fosters conflict. Preparing the budget pitted ministries against one another. Budgeting became a political process of organizing votes to protect a project, a staff position, or a cause. Ministries asked for higher amounts than they needed so that they could survive inevitable reductions as the budget was refined or to cover apportionment shortfalls, so no one had a clear picture of projected costs.

People want more transparency. There were never suspicions of wrongdoing or mismanagement, but most people felt like outsiders to the budgeting process. A limited number of people had a complete financial picture.

When Pathways, our strategic planning task force, began the eighteen-month conversation that led to reorganizing the conference, we knew that any recommendation for change would lack credibility if it didn't address several of these sources of discontent.

Financial Principles

Pathways articulated principles to guide practical recommendations, working with the Council of Finance and Administration (CFA). Some principles found quick consensus; others emerged after considerable deliberation and discussion. What follows is a list of several agreed-upon guidelines.

Insofar as possible, each congregation should bear the costs of its ministry. Except for new church starts or for extraordinary, temporary circumstances, every congregation should pay the entire costs for an appropriate level of clergy leadership without explicit or hidden subsidy from other churches through the apportionments. This includes all costs for health care, pensions, housing, and other benefits.

This principle of returning as many costs as possible to the local church is open to debate. Fundamentally, should congregations be self-sufficient, or should they be subsidized by funds garnered from other churches through apportionments?

Our purpose in adopting this principle isn't to save money or to placate large churches. This approach isn't anticonnectional. Every congregation has the resources to offer ministry appropriate to its size, but most congregations don't have the resources to maintain ministry as they practiced it fifty years ago. Self-sustainability requires facing current reality. The financial stress experienced by many congregations results from trying to sustain a full-time pastor or maintain a large facility with far fewer people than are capable of doing so. If a church spends all its energy to pay the pastor and maintain the facility, it's time to consider part-time ministry, a smaller facility, merger, or some other remedy. Conference subsidies allow such congregations to avoid hard decisions, but they don't enhance ministry. When congregations "right-size," then funds formerly given entirely to salaries and maintenance are freed up for programs and mission. Church leaders can breathe again, and the congregation can reengage its mission field without the constant stress of financial crisis.

Plans that apportion significant parts of clergy support weaken the strongest congregations without strengthening the weakest. What's the right level of pastoral support, a healthy staff configuration, and a sustainable distribution of costs—salaries, programs, facilities, missional giving—for churches of varying sizes and settings? That's the conversation that increases the number of vital congregations of all sizes.

For the long term, focus more on revenue than on costs. The initial impulse of any conference with decreasing revenue and increasing costs is to reduce operating costs immediately. During the recent financial downturn, most US conferences radically cut staff, reduced ministries, and searched for internal efficiencies to lower the budget.

Cutting costs, however, is a short-term solution to a long-term challenge. Reducing staff is a stopgap measure, perhaps an appropriate one as part of resetting priorities, but it offers no long-term solutions. Long-term solutions come from the revenue side of the equation.

This isn't to say that the solution is increasing the budget! Addressing revenue doesn't mean increasing apportionments.

The only long-term sustainable source of revenue results from increasing the number of vital congregations. Revenue doesn't come from conference votes; it comes from congregations that are healthy enough to contribute their share. As long as congregations continue to decline, conference cost cutting offers only short-term relief.

Conferences must reduce costs judiciously and reprioritize budgets to support those ministries that increase the number of vital congregations. Mindless cost cutting or reducing costs to all ministries equally with no evaluation of their importance results in a conference hastening its own decline.

The conference should maximize the resources that remain with local congregations. This may seem to contradict the previous principle, because this requires the conference to reduce costs, eliminate waste, and do whatever else it takes to assure the leanest conference budget so that apportionments remain as low as possible. The primary arena for fulfilling the mission is the local congregation, and the burden rests with the conference to justify why money should be drawn away from congregations. The conference has the obligation to only request support through apportionments that multiply ministries and extend the United Methodist witness.

Insofar as possible, the conference supports congregational self-determination in giving. The apportionment system as practiced in most conferences is a coercive approach to funding ministry. Supervisors reward positive participation and threaten consequences for nonparticipation, and these incentives determine levels of support more than clarity about the missional purpose of the money. The more congregations can give because they want to rather than pay because they have to, the healthier the system becomes. When congregations practice self-determination, then apportionments become an extension of their ministry rather than a franchise fee or tax. Mandated participation deadens enthusiasm, and makes the exercise mechanical and money centered rather than mission focused.

Apportionments should be as simple, fair, and transparent as possible. Every pastor, lay leader, treasurer, and finance committee member should be able to describe what determines the amount of money they are apportioned and how a proposed change in their budget will affect their apportionments in the future.

The budget must reflect the priorities of the conference and focus on fruitfulness. Alignment means matching funding to priorities. Ministries rank first that foster an increase in the number of vital congregations, enhance clergy excellence, and extend the United Methodist witness. All ministries are evaluated by their fruitfulness.

Alternative streams of support can complement the apportionment system. Grants, foundations, personal donations, special gifts, fee-for-services, collaboration with other agencies, and one-time fundraising initiatives are a few of the options to explore.

It's not just a communication problem. When churches express concern about apportionments, conference leaders frequently conclude that if people understood more about how the money is used, the concerns would go away. The conference then invests more heavily in brochures and videos. Transparency is good and communication helps, but the long-term challenge of the apportionment system isn't merely a communication issue, and it's patronizing to suggest it is. When membership continues to decline precipitously while apportionment costs increase, the underlying issues require more than better brochures and videos.

Pathways Recommendations

Pathways worked with CFA to introduce a constellation of tactics intended to align the budget to the mission, reduce costs, increase accountability, and address the sources of discontent. Some tactics took immediate effect, others took years to complete, and others are ongoing.

To create time and space for conversation, the conference took the unusual step of agreeing to a pause on all changes to the budget. From one year to the next, all line items remained constant, all ministries received their same level of support, and all apportionments carried forward without change. The pause interrupted usual patterns of debate, freed the conference from the need to make immediate decisions, and sent a signal that all topics related to finances were open for reconsideration. The pause also provided time for Pathways to complete work related to priorities, expectations, and plans to restructure staff and governance.

The 2006 called session of annual conference adopted a one-page plan presented by Pathways, including the following budget recommendations:

The conference direct bills all pension and health insurance costs to congregations. This alone reduces the conference budget significantly, and shifts costs so that congregations accept responsibility for funding their own pastoral leadership.

Conference policy caps future budget increases. The conference budget can never increase by a percentage that is higher than the percentage change in the aggregate of all church budgets for the previous two years. If church budgets increase by 1 percent, then 1 percent becomes the ceiling for any increases in the conference budget the following year.

Apportionments are determined by operating expenses of local churches over a three-year rolling average. The simple formula allows congregations to anticipate future apportionment costs. When a church increases salaries, operating expenses, or program expenses by 5 percent, leaders can anticipate approximately a 5 percent increase in apportionments in years to come. This varies somewhat since apportionments result from distributing responsibilities relative to other churches, but the formula provides good approximations. The formula excludes membership and attendance numbers, capital expenses, debt service, missional giving, and apportionment giving. By demystifying apportionments, church leaders can consider whether a proposed staff position will stimulate enough new ministry to cover predictable expenses.

The conference reduced apportionments by 25 percent. By direct billing pensions and health insurance, aligning and reducing conference staff, streamlining structure, reducing the size and number of committees, addressing campus ministries, and converting retiree healthcare to a stipend, the budget decreased by more than $3.5 million to $14 million in 2008, which is almost exactly the budget for 2014.

The conference removed apportioned goals and encouraged congregations to support agencies at whatever level they determined. Rather than a centralized, apportioned financial relationship with institutions, the conference invited congregations to cultivate more intimate relationships through service and generosity. Churches are held accountable for the practices of extravagant generosity and risk-taking mission and service, but are free to choose how.

Most of these agencies were originally started by congregations, and for decades these ministries thrived on local financial support and volunteer engagement. They became channels by which churches transformed neighborhoods. During the early 1970s the conference added a line item in the budget to support the college. The next year, another agency was added, and within four years, more than a dozen United Methodist institutions were supported through apportionments. Year by year, the number increased to twenty-eight. The conference took over local congregational responsibility, usurped local self-determination, and separated congregations from their mission field. Voluntary became mandatory; structural connectionalism triumphed over missional connectionalism. The conference voted in 2002 to redesignate most of the line items as goals rather than apportionments, but specific dollar amounts of expected support were still apportioned to every church. Payout settled into a dismal 55 percent, and CFA's previous attempts to change the system were met with great resistance.

Agencies received from $2,000 to $10,000, with a few receiving up to $60,000. A church's apportioned goal might be as little as $6 for one institution and as much as $100 for a larger institution. Many churches paid these nominal amounts without developing any relationship with a ministry.

Apportioned goals limit support rather than fostering contributions. Requiring nine hundred congregations to contribute an aggregate $2,000 seemed inefficient, and did nothing to connect donors to the ministry. Institutions had the impossible task of trying to communicate their message to hundreds of congregations in order to remain on a list that netted them $2,000. The system wasn't working.

After eliminating goals in 2006, the conference monitored giving to ministries that had been supported by goals. Most of the institutions

111

received an immediate boost in funding that later settled into a level of support that was equal or nominally higher than before. As time went on, some ministries thrived under the new approach. For instance, Kingdom House, a UMC community center, received $47,000 in support from the apportioned goals of nearly nine hundred congregations in 2006. Today, a single St. Louis church, The Gathering, has provided more than $180,000 over the last three years, plus hundreds of volunteer hours.

The conference forged a more multifaceted relationship with Central Methodist University. The conference enjoyed a positive relationship with Central Methodist University, a liberal arts college with nearly a thousand students and deep Methodist roots. CMU has provided streams of clergy and lay leadership for Missouri churches. The conference supported CMU with apportionment support of $400,000 to $500,000 that was paid at 70 percent. Each year, support for CMU stimulated heated debate on the floor of annual conference. Alumni, students, and staff lobbied in the hallways to preserve or increase support while opponents prepared petitions to eliminate or reduce support. The political maneuvering divided conference members, harmed the image of CMU among delegates, and generally caused a sense of foreboding about budgetary deliberations. For as long as the CMU debate remained contentious, school administrators couldn't plan with certainty.

The bishop and staff met with the college president and board members for a daylong conversation, which led to several significant changes. First, we agreed that all funding through apportionments would support scholarships for students seeking full-time Christian service. This aligned funding with the mission of the church and removed the objections that some members had to giving apportionments to maintain athletic facilities. Second, the conference agreed to a funding level of $200,000 through apportionments that would remain constant from year to year, allowing administrators to plan ahead with greater certainty. Third, CMU offered a new tuition policy that provides a 50 percent discount for United Methodist students. This assures a robust stream of future United Methodist leaders and long-term healthy ties between the school and the conference. Fourth, the conference publicizes and supports CMU and invites school representatives into churches and youth events. The president addresses annual conference sessions to focus on how CMU extends the United Methodist witness in Missouri and around the world.

These tactics resulted in immediate changes. The percentage of on-campus United Methodist students increased. Due to a number of variables, including a successful capital funds campaign for a student center, CMU's on-campus enrollment increased from 800 to 1,100, while student enrollment in satellite campuses soared to 5,000. CMU has led all UMC-related colleges and universities for the past three years in the number of United Methodist Dollars for Scholars recipients. Contentious debate ceased, administrators plan with greater accuracy, conference funds support scholarships for church-related careers, and congregations welcome campus representatives. Missional clarity has also resulted in a variety of collaborative outcomes that were never anticipated. CMU hosts an annual leadership summit for pastors and laity. CMU, the conference, and two area churches designed an innovative approach to share pastoral leadership and college-age ministries. Participation in college-age ministries has gone from 25 students in 2007 to 120 today.

More United Methodist students, more leadership development, stronger campus ministries, and closer ties to local congregations—these have been fruit of reforging relationships based on more than money.

The conference replaced ineffective, facility-based campus ministries with high expectation, high accountability, congregationally based college-age ministries. More than 350,000 students attend college in Missouri. Thirteen campus ministries funded by $920,000 from apportionments reached only 180 students with worship and 320 in small groups. This was unacceptable and conflicted with the premium we place on fruitfulness and excellence. Pathways recommended a congregationally based model for college-age ministries and prepared a grant process that congregations apply for if they provide a plan and accept benchmarks. The change reduced apportionment support to $400,000. The purpose wasn't merely to reduce costs but to explore a more fruitful process.

In the first year, more than twenty churches applied, and many more churches initiated college-age ministries without conference support. Twenty-five congregations now offer college-age ministries, including thirteen that receive grants, and these reach several times more students than before. An accountability model similar to the Healthy Church Initiative is available. Quality training events are offered regularly for students and leaders.

The conference changed the process by which budgets are prepared. Directors assess priorities with committee chairpersons and staff, receive general guidance from Council of Finance and Administration on the financial status of the conference, and then work together to project costs and prioritize ministries. The directors each meet with CFA to describe the fruit and results of the work of their departments. The Mission Council confirms the proposed budget, and CFA finalizes it and places it before annual conference. The conference eliminated the contentious budgeting process that previously involved dozens of committees.

The conference changes how the budget is presented at annual conference. Previously, the presentation of the budget at annual conference generated numerous questions from the floor as well as motions to amend. Now, delegates receive proposed budgets and recommendations as far in advance as possible. Attention is given to preparing high quality, reliable reports that delegates can read and understand. The CFA chairperson presents the budget and walks through all significant recommendations, describing how changes align with priorities and reflect a focus on fruitfulness. People who have questions or comments are invited to attend a ninety-minute workshop that takes place a day before a final vote is taken. The treasurer and CFA chairperson lead the workshop, answering questions and addressing concerns. Often, more than a hundred people attend the workshop. The chairperson presents the budget for the final vote on the last day of conference, often with no questions since these have been adequately answered in workshops. Adopting the budget takes far less time and offers greater understanding and transparency.

The conference aligns resources according to priorities. The conference budget has two sections: general church support and conference support. All conference support aligns with one of the five centers for which directors are responsible, with priority given to Congregational Excellence and Pastoral Excellence. In addition, conference support includes categories for superintendents, the Board of Ordained Ministry, and the Clergy Support Team. Subcategories within the five centers focus on conference strategies. Each line item aligns to the purpose of the division, and all divisions align with conference priorities and strategies. This contrasts to pre-2005 budgets that had twenty-seven ministry sections each with multiple subsections, plus twenty-eight goals, plus general conference apportionments.

The conference cultivates alternative revenue streams for capital-intensive new church starts, initiatives for clergy excellence, and projects to reach future generations. The bishop and directors engage laity, congregations, and foundations to generate several hundred thousand dollars each year outside the conference budget through a program called Pathways Partners.

The cabinet enforces guidelines for equitable salaries. Congregations receiving equitable salary support must pay their apportionments in full and can't request funding for more than five years. Equitable salary won't be used to prop up declining churches or to provide a full-time salary for a part-time workload in order to maintain an appointment for a pastor. Funds are used to temporarily support a congregation facing short-term financial stress when the church and pastor demonstrate a reasonable expectation of returning to viability and self-sustainability. The use of equitable salary has fallen from over $250,000 to $100,000 annually.

Supervisory conversations about apportionments are directed only to pastors and churches that require it. At the end of each year, the bishop sends letters of appreciation to nearly seven hundred congregations and pastors who give 100 percent or more of their apportionments and a few dozen letters to highlight special efforts by congregations to increase their giving. Only three or four letters are sent to pastors requiring them to bring their chairpersons of finance, pastor-parish relations, and administrative councils to meet with the district superintendent to present a plan for increasing payment during the year to come. Apportionment support is one mark of fruitfulness and health. Supervisory conversations are reserved for situations in which the cabinet perceives an unwillingness to give rather than an inability to give.

The treasurer focuses on congregations. The Pathways recommendations fundamentally changed the role of the Director of Financial and Administrative ministries. The director not only supervises accounting processes but also focuses on helping churches and pastors. The director hosts or leads workshops on generosity, budgeting, stewardship campaigns, internal controls, insurance, salaries, pensions, and other topics to support local churches. The conference staff prepares tool kits, videos, and newsletters with tips on financial ministries and stewardship. The director mentors pastors, travels to churches, and teaches church treasurers.

The fruit of these tactics has been that the conference budget declined by 24.5 percent, from $17,689,000 in 2006 to $13,346,000 in 2009, and the goals of more than $400,000 were eliminated. More churches now give 100 percent or higher of apportionments. The current budget is $13,900,000.

Total contributions to Epworth Family Services, as one example of an agency previously listed as a goal, has increased from $1.2 million to $2.4 million, and volunteer engagement has increased by 30 percent. The conference has led the jurisdiction in Advance giving for three of the last five years, supporting special causes above and beyond apportionment giving. The conference also raised more than one million dollars for disaster relief, gave $500,000 to Nothing but Nets, and pledged more than a million dollars to Imagine No Malaria. Funding for most agencies has increased, some fourfold, the Mozambique Initiative thrives, and overall giving to apportionments has grown from 83.5 percent to 86.5 percent.

A Missionally Aligned Sustainable Strategy

Here is what we've learned as we've worked on financial alignment:

A good budget is based on credible numbers, not rosy scenarios, vague promises, mysteriously optimistic projections, or false trust. If the number of churches and attendees continues to decline and the average age of members continues to increase, the conference loses credibility by increasing apportionments year after year. Adopting budgets that stand no realistic chance of being met erodes trust, and naïve notions that "if we all have faith" or "if we just get all our members to tithe" deny and avoid the hard decisions necessary for long-term viability.

A good budget involves sensible priorities. Anyone looking at the budget should be able to see patterns that distinctly reveal what is most important for the long-term mission of the church. The numbers match the words, values, and purpose of the conference.

A good budget builds self-sustainability into the planning for any new ministry to avoid adding long-term additional costs to the conference that are unrealistic.

A good budget gives credible attention to macroeconomics rather than merely reacting to the internal needs of the conference. It takes into consideration the economic projections, employment figures, and demographic shifts of the larger economy as well as the trends in local church budgets, numbers of churches, ages of pastors, and debt per member ratios.

A good budget moves toward defensible trajectories, putting income and expenditures on pathways that are self-sustaining. Good budgets avoid obvious self-contradictions. For instance, consider the trajectory of a conference with a $13 million budget supported by nine hundred churches if it increases its budget by 3 percent each year while the number of churches and total membership decreases by 3 percent each year. If nothing changes, there will be a day when one hundred churches support a $50 million budget!

A system that relies less on coercion and more on appealing to common values strengthens local church engagement. We have not learned all the lessons we should from the immense success of Nothing but Nets that relied less on centralized, hierarchical enforcement and more on networking, a clear message, and a compelling mission.

Our challenge as United Methodists is less a problem of assets and more an issue of how assets are used. Conferences possess phenomenal resources, but aligning them with the strategies that best reach the mission field requires hard decisions and courage.

It takes years for a conference to break the reflexive habit of adding all worthwhile ministries into the conference budget to be supported by apportionments. The more a conference can avoid this habit, the more missional, voluntary, and energized a project becomes and the more it strengthens congregational ministry.

The apportionment system works well when most churches are growing at a similar rate. It works fairly well when most churches remain stable. However, when only 15 percent of churches are growing, a majority of congregations are declining, and an increasing number are closing, the apportionment system becomes fundamentally unsustainable. As one consultant remarked, "In fifty years, we won't be able to afford our denomination!"

Other Forms of Alignment

A strategy for aligning budgets with the mission has little effect unless the conference aligns other resources as well. Does the conference have the right staff configuration to support the priorities and strategies? Do governance systems support or restrain the mission? Are facilities utilized in a way that reflects the most important tasks? Alignment is about more than finances.

Alignment includes the use of time. Do the bishop, the directors, the superintendents, and lay leaders use their time in a manner that aligns with the fundamental priorities and missional focus of the conference?

Pathways identified two activities that the conference must perform in an exemplary way or else the conference fails in its mission—pastoral excellence and congregational excellence. Conferences fulfill many important functions, but these two are primary.

With this in mind, I try to give 30 percent of my time to work that contributes to strengthening congregations and 30 percent to work that enhances pastoral excellence. (The operative word is try!) Because writing represents an important form for my ministry, I seek to give 20 percent of my time to the task, and the focus of my writing tends to be congregational fruitfulness and clergy excellence. I limit general conference work to 10 percent of my time, mostly attending meetings of the Council of Bishops and the College of Bishops.

The remaining 10 percent of my work goes for all other tasks. The challenge is to squeeze all other work into that remaining 10 percent. The primary benefit of this exercise of assessing time use is to remove, reduce, or avoid tasks that distract from the most important work.

I often fail to meet these goals. But the regular evaluation of time use helps me focus on the most important tasks more than I otherwise would.

In an organization as diffuse and complex as a United Methodist conference, if leaders don't align their time according to priorities, they find themselves doing hundreds of tasks that do nothing to fulfill the essential strategies required to fulfill the mission. Leaders find themselves wonderfully busy, completely exhausted, but totally ineffective.

As an example of shaping time to purpose, I give priority to preaching in churches that are inaugurating new projects rather than churches celebrating anniversaries. I accept invitations to events that have an educational, formative, or missional purpose rather than ceremonial appearances. I attend gatherings focused on learning, innovating, or creating rather than meetings focused on reporting.

John Wesley regularly reflected on the use of time and wrote several sermons on the topic. He realized that how we use our time is how we use our life. Wesley valued intentionality so much that he included admonitions about the use of time in his inquiries for ministerial candidates. "Never trifle away time; neither spend any more time at any one place than is strictly necessary."[2]

Are leaders spending more time on the internal mechanisms of the organizations than on identifying and reaching the mission field? Do they focus too much energy on conflict resolution rather than on cultivating new ministry? Do they invest more time in the 5 percent of clergy who are ineffective than they do confirming and multiplying the capacities of the majority of clergy who are effective?

A strategy for aligning budgets and resources toward the mission is a powerful lever that influences other changes, and yet changing only the financial life of the conference won't reverse decline or reach more people. The challenge is how to make finances transparent, mission driven, and realistic while also keeping financial matters from dominating the life of the conference. Money shouldn't be the most energetically debated topic at annual conference.

Conversation Questions

What values and themes drive your conference's efforts to align budgets toward the mission? How do you feel about the way your conference handles financial issues?

What's the hardest financial decision your conference has made in recent years? What made it difficult? To what extent was the decision mission driven, and how has it affected the ministry of the conference?

What are some of the sources of dissatisfaction in the financial life of your conference? How do these relate to the mission? What suggestions would you make to reframe the conversation?

What principles drive the financial conversation in your conference? What would you add or change?

How clear are you about what influences the amount your congregation is apportioned? How do you see apportioned giving changing in the future?

When has your conference successfully pruned ministries in order to focus more clearly on priorities? What made it work? Why is it so hard for a conference or a church to decide to stop doing something, or to stop doing something the way it has always been done?

What would sustained obedience in a consistent direction look like for your conference, and how would this affect your conference's decisions about money?

How does the time leaders give to various issues, programs, and ministries reflect the priorities of the conference? How do you monitor your own use of time and how it supports the mission of your church or conference?

The Sixth Lever

A STRATEGY FOR CREATING TECHNICALLY ELEGANT GOVERNANCE SYSTEMS

A university is governed by a board of trustees that relates to the president and senior staff. A company is led by a board of directors that works with a CEO and company officers. In contrast, a United Methodist conference disperses responsibility for basic governance across a number of committees and staff, including a board of trustees to handle property and insurance, a council on finance to oversee funds and budgets, and a conference council to coordinate programs and to connect ministries. This stream of leadership derives its authority from the annual conference when it meets in yearly sessions. The bishop, cabinet, and superintendents operate in a parallel leadership stream to supervise and appoint pastors and to work with congregations.

With authority so diffusely distributed, how does a conference form a governing center to provide direction and accountability for the mission of the church?

Governance

Governance, a word seldom used to describe conference operations, refers to the system of boards, committees, and leadership an organization uses to provide direction, oversight, and administration of its work. Governing boards maintain accountability and provide independence, guaranteeing voice and influence from the laity, pastors, and congregations who supply the resources and are affected by the decisions of the conference. Governance is the internal skeleton that provides structure for the corporate body. Agreed-upon policies or standing rules distribute responsibility and accountability. The fundamental tasks of governance are the same for universities, companies, and nonprofits.

The first task of governance is to focus the organization on its primary mission, to "cradle the vision" as some say. A governing body defines, refines, extends, and limits the mission to unify all constituent components, to set direction and priority, and to mobilize people for work that contributes to the mission. Governing boards hold leaders accountable for the mission and align resources for the task.

Second, an effective governing board pushes the whole organization to focus outwardly and presses leaders and staff to look to the needs of those they seek to serve. Peter Drucker writes, "An organization begins to die the day it begins to operate for the benefit of the insiders and not the benefit of the outsiders."[1]

The church fulfills its mission at the margins of the congregation, where those who actively follow Christ encounter those who aren't a part of the community of faith. Picture a congregation as concentric circles. In the center circle are the pastor, the leaders and staff, and key volunteers who plan and think and pray and act to lead the church. Farther out is the circle that includes other leaders, including teachers, volunteers, and helpers, and then another circle for those who attend and participate in worship, work projects, and Bible studies. The next larger circle includes all those who attend with less consistency.

When we reach the edge of the farthest circle, we discover on the other side of the margin the people who are not part of the community of faith. The church fulfills its mission at that edge, where those who belong to the community engage and interweave their lives with those outside the community. There, at the margin, we fulfill our mission, through *service and justice* ministries—helping, serving, relieving suffering—and through *our sharing the goods news of Christ*—seeking, inviting, welcoming, and nurturing faith. In a missional church, the boundary is wonderfully permeable, and members reach across the edge and new people easily enter into the faith community. The mission of the church isn't fulfilled in church planning meetings composed of church members talking with other members about church business, although those meetings may be important to strategize about the mission. The margin is where the action is.

We can also view a conference as concentric circles. In the center circle are the bishop, cabinet, staff, and elected volunteers who work in positions of leadership. In the next larger circle are those who serve on conference committees and attend annual conference, and in the largest circle are all the pastors and congregations that belong to conference. It's not in the conference center that the conference fulfills its mission but at the margins where congregations engage the world around them. The mission of the church isn't fulfilled in conference offices or committees, although these might be important for strategy and planning. Talkers become doers, and our mission in Christ becomes incarnate at the margins.

Jesus focused his attention on the margins of the community, usually over the objection of the religious leaders of his day and the counsel of his followers. Nearly every gospel story involves Jesus speaking with the marginalized: calling tax collectors, healing lepers, engaging a woman at the well, interceding on behalf of a woman accused of adultery, receiving children, challenging moneychangers, praying with a thief on the cross. We have no stories of Jesus attending meetings! When he does gather his disciples, he draws their attention to the people at the margins: "'I assure you that when you have done it for one of the least of these brothers and sisters of mine, you have done it for me" (Matt 25:40).

A critical role of leadership is to constantly draw the attention of the conference to the margins where the mission is fulfilled. Leading means outward-focused thinking. Who is our neighbor, locally and globally, and what does God call us to do? Early Methodist conferences refreshed pastors and laity for the mission field. Conference was a means of reinvigorating one another for continued engagement with the mission field. The systems developed by Wesley and the early Methodists propelled energy outward. Francis Asbury, in a journal entry about the itineracy in 1797, writes, "We must draw resources from center to circumference."[2] Effective governance focuses on the needs and opportunities of the mission field.

Third, a governing board forces future-oriented thinking. It stays attuned to the culture, anticipates trends, notices threats, and focuses on sustainability. It watches trajectories, takes the long view on issues related to personnel and the use of resources and property, and evaluates the usefulness of strategies and operations. It helps the organization to change and adapt, to remain relevant and effective. An effective governing board refuses to avoid the difficult challenges. It thinks about next generations, fosters innovation, and assures long-term continuance of the mission.

Finally, a governing board stays connected to its base, to those who elected its members and authorized their work. It communicates with its constituencies and invites their participation in the mission. It can't become isolated from the people most invested, especially the laity, clergy, and congregations of the conference.

Technically Elegant

The words "technically elegant" may bring to mind the sleekest new mobile phone with the most fantastic features, but let's use it instead to describe better administration in a complex organization. What makes governance technically elegant?[3]

A technically elegant governance system is user-friendly, intuitively understandable, simple, and effective. It solves numerous critical communication issues. It accomplishes the mission, and aligns personal, financial, and organizational resources.

A technically elegant system works smoothly for the people who participate in it rather than frustrating and exhausting them. It releases the talent and the ideas of people rather than restraining or stifling them. It provides the best conditions for people to offer themselves for leadership and to bear fruit.

In a technically elegant administrative system, people are clear about who does what, and they operate without undue territoriality or defensiveness. People know what resources are available to them and to whom they are accountable. People important for a decision aren't left out of the loop, and projects don't get stuck by an expectation of complete consensus.

All committees and staff have a direct line of sight between the work they do and the mission of the conference, the work of the churches, and the ministry of Christ. They have a sense of where the conference is going as a whole, and how their task fits into the larger picture.

Technically elegant systems connect people to work collaboratively on large objectives and minimize activities that are irrelevant, nonproductive, or unnecessary. They optimize organizational relationships. People work together who most need to do so, and teams are able to make decisions without excessive bureaucratic layers of permission seeking. Information flows efficiently—vertically and horizontally—and reaches those first who most need it to do their work. Technically elegant systems attract and select excellent leadership, people who are knowledgeable, talented, and effective in their area of expertise.

Consequently, such systems foster deliberate and thorough decision making in a timely manner so that the organization remains agile enough to respond to opportunities quickly.

This describes an unreachable ideal, and no system works so perfectly. And yet describing technical elegance gives us something to aim for.

Two Streams of Authority

A strategy for technically elegant governance doesn't require aligning every single one of the hundreds of components of conference operations, but it must interweave the most critical streams of authority and work.

The first challenge results from the fact that authority in a United Methodist conference flows through two distinct streams.

One stream of authority flows through the bishop's office, the bishop's support staff, the district superintendents and their offices, to the pastors and churches through supervision and conducting charge conferences. This "cabinet stream" deploys and supervises clergy, works directly with congregational leaders, and provides programs at the district level.

The other stream of authority flows through the conference council, conference staff, and elected boards and committees to provide programs. Most components of the "conference stream" are directed by the *Book of Discipline*, which defines the purpose and composition of councils and boards. The conference stream administers staff, sets budgets, oversees property and insurance, and provides structure for dozens of programs, such as conference youth ministries, campus ministries, camping, social action, mission, disaster response, safe sanctuaries, lay leadership, and many more. The bishop presides at annual conference and superintendents serve on conference boards, but the disciplinary relationships between the two streams are fewer and weaker than most people realize.

Conferences vary on how these two distinct streams interrelate. In some conferences, the bishop doesn't share the same building as conference staff. Some conferences consider any initiative by the bishop or cabinet to influence budgets or shape priorities as intrusive. Bishops don't attend council meetings, seldom participate in budget conversations, never work directly with the Board of Ordained Ministry, and play a minor role in selecting conference staff.

In other conferences, the bishop and cabinet enjoy a mutually supportive relationship with conference staff and boards, but they seldom involve themselves in operational details. Bishops are treated as guests, but they don't shape agendas or deliberate on administrative issues.

In still other conferences, the two streams of authority flow together with multiple points of collaboration and interaction. Bishops and superintendents serve on conference boards while conference directors serve as members of the cabinet.

Even in the best examples of collaboration, the dual streams create stress. District programs clash with conference calendars; conference staff tangle with district personnel about deadlines and forms; superintendents feel left out when conference staff engage churches in their district without their knowledge.

The first major challenge for creating technically elegant governance systems is to integrate these two streams of authority to work in the most advantageous way for the mission of the conference. This is no simple task. The *Discipline* encourages (and nearly engenders) silos, even though the evidence of best practices supports efforts to unify and collaborate. These streams must flow toward a healthy confluence.

The Conference Council

The second challenge is that a common model conferences use to govern—the conference council—performs poorly and isn't conducive to strategic decision making, thorough deliberation, or leading the conference to face its adaptive challenges. This isn't to blame anyone—conference directors, members of the council, or those who serve as officers of the council. The model itself doesn't work well, even with the best leadership and planning.

The conference council as envisioned by the *Discipline,* if we were to follow every paragraph that mandates or recommends functions and membership, is too large, too unfocused, too preoccupied with its own operations, and too unwieldy to provide a place for focused, strategic, or innovative work. In conferences where the council seems to function well, a closer examination reveals that most work takes place in smaller groups and that the council principally serves a communication role. Congregations discovered the redundant and limiting effect of a council of ministries decades ago, and most abandoned the model for more streamlined administrative councils.

The size of conference councils can extend to fifty or more people, and this makes deliberative, thorough conversations impossible. The *Discipline* places a premium on representing every ministry, meaning that chairpersons from dozens of boards and committees may comprise the council. Attention is given to representation by district, age, gender, ethnicity, clergy or lay status, and this multiplies the size of the membership. Staff is present as well as cabinet representatives, lay leaders, and representatives of UM-related institutions.

The representational nature of the council means that each member filters decisions through the lens of the constituency he or she represents, asking, "What's the impact on my committee or district or ministry? How can I promote the work of my team?" Redirection of resources toward one area elicits a reaction from other constituents who demand to be treated equally, and this makes strategic alignment nearly impossible. The model places people in an unintended competitive and defensive posture that makes budgets difficult to negotiate.

The conference council, because of its size and composition, becomes primarily a reporting organization instead of a learning organization. Each constituency describes what it has done or plans to do, but there isn't time to drill down to critical issues. Councils spend more time on events that have already happened than they do on future challenges. They focus on matters that are significant to individual components of the conference but that have no significant bearing on the conference as a whole. They suffer from a short-term bias, focused on what will happen next month rather than upon positioning the conference for the future. They operate reactively, responding to plans brought to them by constituent groups rather than by initiating larger strategies that derive from the mission. As one frustrated member said, "We report, review, rehash, and redo the same work that staff and committees have already done."

Additionally, the council is disconnected from the other major stream of authority that flows through the bishop's office and cabinet. The council may invest considerable energy in projects that receive little support from the bishop and cabinet or may ignore priorities identified and championed by the bishop and cabinet as essential to the mission.

Finally, the council requires immense amounts of time and energy to operate. It dissipates energy rather than focusing it, and this makes the model cumbersome and inefficient.

A risk of regularly gathering all the people assigned by the *Discipline* to serve on the council for daylong meetings or lengthy retreats is that the church becomes too focused on its inner life and inner workings. We think we've accomplished something because we have prepared a report, attended a meeting, or passed a resolution. All our signs of success are internal, and we congratulate ourselves for affecting the inner workings of the church rather than for changing the lives of people outside the church. Large, tightly regulated representational models for governance create their own gravitational pull that draws energy inward rather than focusing attention outward.

Most United Methodist conferences have adapted the traditional conference council by making changes as allowed by the *Discipline*. Some have made minor adjustments, and others have radically reorganized their operations while remaining faithful to the *Discipline*'s mandates for vertical alignment that connects general boards to conference and local church ministries.

Conferences that substantially change structures still face challenges that result from the long legacy of working from a conference council model. The model raised the expectation of egalitarianism, that every group deserves the same attention, time, and access to resources as every other group. Or it fostered the notion that no initiative can move forward unless every constituency has participated in preparing it. Unless everybody agrees, nothing happens.

Finding the Right People

A third challenge for a strategy for better governance is finding the right people to serve in leadership. The people who serve in paid positions as directors, as superintendents, in specialized ministries, or as support staff must be selected with the highest attention to expertise, experience, and fruitfulness. Nothing communicates an organization's values more clearly than its selection of leadership. Trust throughout a conference derives from how people perceive the motivations and competence of conference staff and superintendents. These positions can't serve as placeholders for people whose competencies make them impossible to appoint elsewhere. Appointments must be made based on competency. Spiritual groundedness, a pattern of fruitful ministry, an ability to work well with people, openness to accountability, excellence in their area of expertise—these are the qualities that staff must exhibit.

In addition, the conference must provide a nominations system that identifies high-quality lay and clergy volunteers and places them in positions that match their gifts and expertise. Nothing distracts purposeful work for a team as significantly as members who are driven by personal agendas, given to conflict, insistent on having their own way, or unfamiliar with the basic knowledge required to participate in the group.

Teams make better decisions when they are comprised of a diverse mix of people who reflect the diverse, multiethnic, multicultural mission field we serve. On the other hand, rigidly applying requirements that put geographic, gender, ethnic, age, or church-size diversity before expertise

128

results in choosing people who have no interest, passion, or experience for the work, and this has a deadening effect on operations.

An Experimental Approach

In order to address these various challenges, the Missouri Conference adopted an organizational plan that formed a smaller Mission Council to fulfill the principal governing purposes of the conference council and a personnel structure with five conference directors leading and coordinating work. The plan borrows elements from several other annual conferences that have undergone similar reorganizations.

The plan has worked well. It fits the temperament and gifts of current leadership, fulfills the principal purposes of governance, and appears user-friendly, simple, and effective. Most importantly, the plan interweaves the two major streams of authority into a unified effort that has helped us accomplish remarkable change and better align our personnel and financial resources. This plan isn't for every conference, however, and each conference needs to explore governance solutions that match its culture and that fit the leadership style of its bishop, staff, and elected officers.

The Mission Council

Operationally, three interrelated gatherings administer the work of the conference—the Mission Council, the cabinet, and a directors meeting. We didn't know in 2007 that this pattern would emerge when we adopted a plan for reorganizing the conference. The plan created the Mission Council and identified five areas of work for the directors, but the practice of governing through three interrelated gatherings took years to evolve.

The Mission Council gives general direction, guidance, and alignment of resources to support the mission. It focuses on cultivating vibrant, fruitful, growing congregations that change lives for Jesus Christ. Its primary questions are the following: Are we leading congregations to lead people to actively follow Jesus Christ? What outcomes help us determine whether we are accomplishing our mission? What shall we do to more effectively fulfill this mission? The Mission Council derives its authority from annual conference and acts on behalf of annual conference between sessions on matters not limited by the *Discipline*.

The Mission Council has thirteen voting members, a majority of whom are laity, and seven nonvoting members, including the five directors, the bishop, and a district superintendent. The conference lay leader, as well as the chairpersons of finance; ordained ministry; congregational development; and mission, service, and justice ministries are the only five voting members serving by virtue of their office. Membership reflects the diversity of the conference. The bishop provides leadership for the Mission Council, either by presiding over the meetings without vote or inviting someone else to preside.

The Mission Council convenes six times a year in meetings that include two hours of business, reporting, and communication; a lunch break; and ninety minutes to process a critical issue, to discuss an essay or book, or to explore an innovation that the conference is considering.

The agenda of the Mission Council focuses on the work of the five directors, the lay leader, and the cabinet. Members ask questions, offer suggestions and support, and learn about upcoming opportunities in the five principal areas of the conference's work. Directors report on the committees that relate to their work. Conversations are rigorous, and directors honestly describe challenges, critical issues, or trends. Members shape policy, provide feedback, and offer alternative solutions. Since the Mission Council assigns day-to-day management of the annual conference to the directors, few actual votes are taken by the council. Directors are held accountable for the operations of the conference.

Since the majority of the voting members are laity, the Mission Council provides the principal form of lay investment and engagement in governance for the conference. Lay persons influence outcomes and give feedback to the directors, the cabinet, and the bishop. They also interpret the work of the Mission Council to the committees and communities where they serve.

To enhance the quality of conversation, members of the Mission Council are sent an agenda, the preliminary reports from directors, and a budget summary in advance of meetings so that they have adequate time to prepare. The actual conduct of the meeting is conversational and focuses on learning, problem solving, and exploring ways to improve conference ministries. It's outward focused and future oriented and always grounded in an awareness of the missional needs of the communities. The group is small enough to delve deeply into critical issues and yet large enough to provide a wide range of perspectives from lay and clergy from churches of varying sizes and contexts. Attendance is high, and conversation is lively. Members believe that their work matters, their opinions are heard, and their participation makes a difference.

The Cabinet

The second of the three interrelated gatherings that administer the work of the conference is the cabinet. The cabinet comprises nine district superintendents, five conference directors, the lay leader, and the bishop. It convenes for a day and a half once a month from September through January, for a three day assessment retreat in February, and for eight two-day sessions during March, April, and May.

The composition of the cabinet has evolved. Originally, only superintendents and the bishop met as a cabinet. Occasionally, conference directors were invited to join the superintendents for a meeting of the "extended cabinet."

When the conference redefined the role of directors during restructuring, the directors became far more engaged with congregations and pastoral formation. Directors know the intricacies of congregational work and pastoral leadership as well as superintendents but from a different vantage point. They have become primary resources for superintendents. Superintendents rely upon their counsel and invite them to help with critical situations just as directors rely upon superintendents to connect them with the churches that need their resources. Directors serve in superintendent-level positions, with equivalent salary, benefits, and access to the bishop. The work of superintendents and directors became so intertwined that when the cabinet met, superintendents needed information that was known by one or more of the directors. We now define cabinet as the superintendents, the directors, and the lay leader, and we no longer use the term *extended cabinet*.

Including the directors as members of the cabinet has proven to be the single most significant step toward creating the confluence between conference operations and cabinet responsibilities. A typical cabinet agenda includes worship and reports from the directors and lay leader and then delves into critical personnel, congregational, or missional issues. The primary role of superintendents is to empower pastors and churches for the mission rather than to audit them, measure them, and report on them. Most cabinet meetings include two or more hours of learning time or "balcony time" to discuss a book or to explore a potential ministry.

Our use of directors as specialists to resource churches caused us also to rethink the role of superintendent, shifting the focus more toward mission strategist and less toward administration and conflict management. One superintendent was appointed to the position of assistant to the bishop for leadership development, relinquishing the title of superintendent but remaining on the cabinet. He serves as dean of the cabinet and supplements the work of superintendents to address critical situations and strategic opportunities, such as strengthening midsize churches. Nine superintendents serve twelve districts, with the support of the five directors and the assistant to the bishop. This hybrid system honors the *Discipline*, which requires superintendents to serve geographic areas, while allowing the cabinet the flexibility to focus expertise strategically as needed.

The Directors Meeting

The third of the three interrelated gatherings that administer the work of the conference is the directors meeting. The directors of congregational excellence; pastoral excellence; connectional ministries; finance and administrative ministries; and mission, service, and justice ministries—these five persons oversee all conference operations.

Directors meet monthly together with the bishop to keep one another apprised of their work, to collaborate, coordinate calendars, address critical issues, and strategize together. Directors work interactively week in and week out, clustering in subgroups, exchanging information, and soliciting counsel from one another. They step into one another's offices frequently to coordinate work. The directors work with the bishop to prepare the agenda for the Mission Council.

The interchange between directors fosters the horizontal flow of information across departments, transfers best practices, breaks through staff silos, provides mutual support, and results in economies of scale as directors coordinate support staff. Directors work as a team on every major conference project. The directors prepare and present a unified proposed budget to the finance committee and the Mission Council.

The directors are deeply engaged with churches and pastors. Along with the superintendents, they act as the chief tacticians of the conference, putting strategies into practice and giving programmatic expression to goals. They serve as catalysts for change and stimulate outward-focused ministry.

Directors supervise all other staff, providing vertical alignment. The bishop rarely second-guesses a director's decision, and directors have significant latitude and authority to act in their areas of responsibility.

The Mission Council has the formal authority to make decisions on behalf of the annual conference. In practice, major decisions are filtered through all three gatherings, the directors meeting, the cabinet, and the council before action is taken. This gives ample opportunity to discuss, deliberate, amend, and refine proposals and to involve lay leadership, conference staff, and the cabinet. This plan also allows the organization to act quickly, usually in six to eight weeks, on significant initiatives.

This approach weaves the two major streams of authority into a more unified governance system without losing the oversight of independent elected lay and clergy representing the conference. It fulfills the mandated vertical alignment as general board functions are represented at the Mission Council and through conference committees. The close collaboration between laity, cabinet, and directors reduces conflicting messages sent through the system. It provides three distinct settings for deliberative work that are small enough to be effective and large enough to represent diverse constituencies. It pushes day-to-day decisions deeper into the organization, allowing the Mission Council to focus on long-term directional decisions. It fosters initiative and allows leaders to act without undue delays or endless levels of permission seeking. And rather than a tight command and control atmosphere, this approach cultivates an invitational, conversational, and collaborative process.

In Practice

How does an idea move from creative spark to fruition? With a technically elegant system, the governing board is clear about purpose and priorities, and it clarifies larger strategies, strategies that give permission throughout the system for innovation and experimentation. The most likely sources of tactical ideas that put strategies into practice are churches, pastors, teams, and task forces at the margins.

It surprises people that no "official board" ever voted on the Healthy Church Initiative, a major program of the Missouri Conference. HCI began as an experiment with a small group of clergy working with their superintendent. Because of the good results, a director invited a task force to expand the plan. The Congregational Development Team redirected funds for training. Progress was reported through the Mission Council and the cabinet, and plans were refined by these groups. The experiment grew and was given a name. HCI expanded and was given higher visibility since it fulfills a major priority of the conference to increase the number of vital congregations. Superintendents embraced the program and encouraged churches to participate. Directors formed another task force to explore a parallel program for small churches and then later another to focus on college-age ministries, and these resulted in the Small Church Initiative and College-Age Ministries Initiative. The Mission Council, the cabinet, and the directors meetings regularly receive reports on progress, costs, and outcomes.

The Healthy Church Initiative could not have originated and come to fruition in a conference board of discipleship composed and tasked according to the *Discipline*. Nor could HCI have been forced into a standard board of discipleship after the program was developed. Beginning with disciplinary mandates seldom works and usually results in merely repeating ministries that were offered the previous year. A ministry that begins experimentally at the margins and successfully meets real needs inevitably requires its own unique support system.

People and Processes

A system can't operate more effectively than the people who participate in it. If the nominations process is flawed, then the whole system struggles with consistency, effectiveness, and focus. The conference nominations process plays a critical role. The nominations committee changed how it identifies and invites leadership. The committee develops an extensive pool of people, every one of which has been proposed by someone for their spiritual maturity, commitment, and expertise. Each person is contacted personally and invited to complete a spiritual gifts inventory online, and each must agree to serve actively if invited to do so. This creates a pool of hundreds of prospective leaders. The nominations committee then forms teams based on expertise, interest, and ability, with attention to gender, ethnic, age, geographical, and lay/clergy diversity. Without changing our nominating processes, our organizational structure wouldn't work.

Identifying and eliminating duplicative committees with unclear tasks and ill-defined relationships is essential. Some of the established ways are set up for failure and frustration, and these sap the energy of leaders and erode trust. Consolidating similar functions into single units strengthens effectiveness.

Staff who overfunction leave the volunteers who serve on committees with nothing to do but rubber-stamp work already underway. This disenfranchises leaders and makes governance perfunctory. On the other hand, staff who remain passive, underengaged, or unprepared cause committees to drift into purposelessness.

Reducing redundant committees and using fewer people in formal leadership streamlines operations. The use of task forces and think tanks increases engagement, energy, and expertise. The conference now has half as many people in formally elected leadership, but it invites twice as many people into task forces or ministry teams than ever before. Ministry motivates people more than meetings.

The plan works because it fits the temperament, gifts, and leadership styles of the bishop, the directors, and the lay leadership of the conference. Different contexts require different approaches, so long as the essential functions of governance are fulfilled effectively. This plan intertwines the two strands of authority that every conference governance system must address if it is to bring focus to the mission. It's faithful to the *Discipline* by placing final authority in an elected council that is predominantly lay, amenable to the annual conference, and vertically aligned with the work of the general church. It distributes more authority toward the leadership of the bishop and the directors than most systems, and that is its strength and a source of criticism.

Many conferences are experimenting with alternative systems of governance, and we have much to learn from these. Innovation doesn't move through the fifty-seven US conferences like an arrowhead with one conference or two out front, a few right behind, and the rest following from there. Rather, progress moves like an amoeba, as one conference inches forward here and another there and a third over there.

A successful strategy for better governance won't solve the decline of the church, the aging of our membership, or any of the other major challenges that threaten our mission. However, the task of leading becomes immeasurably more difficult with governance systems that don't work well and that aren't conducive to our mission. Getting this lever right positions the other levers to work better. Technical elegance may be elusive, but it's worth striving for.

Leaders who experiment to find systems that are more conducive to our mission join a long line of innovators. John Wesley and the early Methodists continually tried new approaches to organize their work, improving, refining, and experimenting. Our attention to Wesley's fastidious requirements for reporting, regulating, and providing discipline sometimes blinds us to the bold initiative, creative imagination, and expansive view of ministry that gave rise to the circuit system, classes, bands, societies, preaching houses, publishing, lay stewards, superintendent ministers, and the formation of conference. These innovations were driven by missional necessity, the same mission that drives our need for better systems today.

Conversation Questions

If you have served on a conference board or observed the work of a conference council, what was the experience like? What are the positive and fruitful aspects of conference administration, and what do you find frustrating and confusing?

How user-friendly and intuitively understandable is your governance system? How smoothly does it work for the people who serve in positions of leadership as volunteers or staff?

What are the principal governing components of your conference, and how well do they do at focusing the attention of the conference on the mission? How does your conference force future-oriented thinking and maintain an outward focus?

Describe how the two streams of authority work in your conference. What fosters confluence, cooperation, and communication between the authority derived from the bishop's office and the authority derived from conference staff and boards? What points of tension or disconnection seem problematic? What suggestions would you make?

Complexity is the silent killer of organizations. What does this mean for you?

Can you think of a few simple changes in conference operations that would have a multiplying and positive effect? How would you improve your conference's governance systems?

How does your conference learn? How well does it adopt new models or introduce change?

The Seventh Lever

A STRATEGY FOR RECONFIGURING
CONFERENCE SESSIONS

Imagine gathering for three days of annual conference without conducting any business or taking any votes. No budgets to approve and no reports to receive. No standing rules to adopt and no resolutions to debate. No petitions to present and no task forces to appoint. No boards to elect and no motions to amend. What would we do for three days?

When we perceive annual conference as principally a business session, then it's a waste of time and money if we conduct no business. Someone might suggest that we skip annual conference altogether.

On the other hand, imagine gathering lay and clergy from all the congregations together in one place to reconfirm who we are, what we do, and why it matters. Imagine high-quality worship, preaching, teaching, and service that clarify our common mission, reconnect us with one another, stimulate best practices, renew our spirits, and help us rededicate ourselves to Christ and to the people God calls us to serve. What an opportunity to remind ourselves of our work together as followers of Christ in the Wesleyan way, to integrate new pastors and lay leaders into our community, and to encourage one another in the task of ministry.

It makes no sense to gather hundreds of people merely to adopt a budget. Why settle for a business meeting when annual conference can be so much more?

The seventh lever is a strategy to reconfigure annual conference sessions so that our time together clarifies, connects, equips, and encourages. When conferences shift from meetings to ministry, from reporting to learning, from debating to best practices, then they energize, revive, and remind. They teach and embolden. They focus the attention of churches toward the mission field. They cultivate the call and draw people into projects that transform the world. Annual conference provides the best single platform to stimulate change and to multiply the impact of congregations.

Originally, conferences conducted none of the business we now associate with them. They convened for other purposes. The practice of conferencing became a critical element of our Methodist identity and a powerful missional tool for reasons other than budgets and reports.

Wesley's Conference

How did the notion of conferring together (conference!) begin for United Methodists? John Wesley describes the first conference this way:

> In June, 1744, I desired my brother and a few other clergymen to meet me in London, to consider how we should proceed to save our own souls and those that heard us. After some time, I invited lay preachers that were in the house to meet with us. We conferred together for several days, and were much comforted and strengthened thereby. The next year I not only invited most of the traveling preachers but several others to confer with me in Bristol. . . . This I did for many years, and all that time the term Conference meant not so much the conversations we had together, as the persons who conferred.[1]

The agenda for the first conference was threefold. Mr. Wesley and the Methodists conferred on "1. What to teach, 2. How to teach, and 3. What to do, that is, how to regulate our doctrine, discipline, and practice."[2]

According to Russell E. Richey's *The Methodist Conference in America*, early conferences comprised a family of preachers and church leaders held together by affection, common rules, a shared mission, and a watchfulness of the members over one another.[3] They were strongly relational, providing mutual support and encouragement, and they were purpose driven, focused on how to extend the gospel message in ever more fruitful ways. Far from merely serving a business function, they served as the spiritual center of Methodism. They dealt with the training and deployment of pastors, and they pooled their resources to provide for common ministries to address needs beyond the scope of any local congregation.

Conferences mobilized people for ministry. They were a time to reinforce identity, to teach, and to plan how to go forward. Far from dreary reports, arguments over budgets, and amendments to amendments, conferences served as a critical strategy to multiply ministry and to keep communication and connection alive.

The business aspects are important. But too great a focus on reports and budgets distracts from the original missional intent of conference. The challenge is how to conduct required business with integrity, transparency, and effectiveness while also providing an experience that unifies, inspires, motivates, and equips.

Desired Outcomes

In his book, *The Advantage: Why Organizational Health Trumps Everything Else in Business*, Patrick Lencioni describes the need for clarity of purpose for organizations. When leaders can agree to and rally around clear answers to certain fundamental questions—without using jargon or smarmy language—they drastically increase the health of the organization. Among those questions are the following:

1. Why do we exist?
2. How do we behave?
3. What do we do?
4. How will we succeed?[4]

The goal isn't to have a perfect answer to each question but to have an answer that is directionally correct and to which people can commit. While the bishop and conference leaders may answer these questions in their own personal ways, the general direction and priorities should agree.

In the Missouri Conference, the answer to the first question involves our denomination's mission statement and our agreement that the conference "leads congregations to lead people to actively follow Jesus Christ." The five expectations—Christ-centered, fruitfulness, excellence, accountability, and collaboration—provide underlying values to answer question two. Our core process that focuses on congregational excellence and pastoral excellence gives direction to our work and suggests an answer to question three. The seven strategies outlined in this book provide the basis for conversation and planning for question four.

Answers to these questions aren't arbitrarily given by a single leader; they emerge from reflection and conversation across the conference. For

Missouri, answers to the first three questions were formalized through the adoption of the Pathways recommendations.

Refining answers to these questions belongs to everyone who holds leadership in the conference, and it's a continuing task. But the task doesn't end when a few leaders come to consensus. Lencioni writes about the importance of fostering clarity as deeply and broadly in the organization as possible.

Can a majority of the members of annual conference answer these questions with enough consistency to bring direction to conversations and work? Annual conference sessions provide a critical forum for bringing just such clarity.

This is exactly what Wesley was doing during his first conferences. He addressed fundamental questions of purpose, value, and strategy. What are we to teach, how are we to teach it, and what standards apply? Wesley reinforced clarity of mission and mobilized people to next steps.

Annual conference sessions can bring clarity of purpose more deeply into the life of the conference. This isn't to suggest that bishops hammer conference members with overworked mission statements or simple-minded slogans. Polite, kind, well-crafted slogans that aren't genuine or believable or which are effusively earnest, overgeneralized aspirations, do more harm than good. Rather, leaders and planners should intend for preaching, worship, teaching, fellowship, and the business of annual conference to contribute to answering and reinforcing the fundamental purposes of Christ, the church, and the annual conference in ways that resonate with our theology, identity, purpose, and context.

Leaving organizational theory aside, how might we describe the desired outcomes of annual conference sessions?

We hope that members of annual conference drive away thinking, "I'm glad I was here, and I hope I get to come again next year," that people feel like they've spent their time well, and that they're doing work that matters.

We hope the quality of worship, preaching, and teaching models excellence.

We pray that members leave annual conference clearer about our mission and more confident about our future, and that people understand the purpose, work, and strategies of conference.

We hope people learn practices and approaches that strengthen their skills as leaders in their congregations.

We hope people leave feeling more connected, more deeply interwoven into the larger fabric of United Methodist witness, more knowledgeable about resources to strengthen their ministries, and more ready to ask for help.

We hope people feel inspired, encouraged, and challenged to a deeper commitment to Christ and that the experience of annual conference confirms and fosters a calling to ministry.

We hope that the fundamental business of annual conference is completed with integrity and effectiveness and without acrimony.

We hope that annual conference draws the attention of churches toward the mission field and reinforces future-oriented thinking.

To the extent annual conference succeeds with these outcomes, people become clearer about how to answer Lencioni's questions, and the conference operates with greater health.

Tactics for Purposeful Sessions

Many conferences across the connection have already made significant changes in the way they conduct annual conference sessions, using a variety of tactics to shift from mere business to events that clarify, connect, equip, and encourage. We've learned much from other conferences, borrowing ideas and experimenting with new approaches as we sharpen our own strategy. What follows are some tactics that have been helpful for us to identify and name:

A clear, compelling theme. A principal tactic involves identifying a clear, compelling theme that shapes the entire event. A good theme derives from the mission of the conference but focuses on a specific element of that purpose. A theme drives the work of planning teams, shapes the agenda and design elements, determines which guest speakers we invite and what workshops we offer, provides direction for preachers and worship leaders, and establishes the priority that will shape the entire year, including charge conferences following annual conference.

A recent theme for Missouri's annual conference was *Praying Hands and Dirty Fingernails,* taken from an essay by the same title in *Remember the Future.*[5] The theme celebrated Wesley's uniting personal piety with social holiness and provided a platform for teaching about prayer, spiritual formation, and faith development that feeds ministries that serve the poor, relieve suffering, and seek justice. A devotional was sent to members before annual conference; a guest writer led sessions on prayer, and a prayer room and labyrinth were made available. Another guest speaker launched our Imagine No Malaria campaign; we renewed our Mozambique Initiative partnerships, held a 5-K run and a UMW walk for mission, built a Habitat House, and sent several hundred volunteers into the community for service projects. Twenty workshops taught best practices related to spiritual formation or outreach for congregations, and sermons resonated with the theme. Fall charge conferences followed up with Imagine No Malaria.

Another recent theme, *Louder Than Before,* focused on reaching next generations. Special guests included the authors Kenda Creasy Dean and Chuck Bomar. Youth led a Friday night street party. Four hundred youth joined in sessions, and workshops were tailored to youth ministries. Young people participated in a panel discussion with the bishop, and the ordination service included stories of the call to ministry with music led by youth. Charge conferences focused on reaching unchurched youth.

Selecting a compelling theme may seem so self-evident that it deserves little attention. The challenge is maintaining the discipline to focus energy, resources, and personnel on the theme in a manner that actually impacts congregations and church leaders. Some conferences don't let the theme drive the event. They invite a guest to speak but allow the rest of conference to be driven by competing topics, priorities, and agendas. Following through with a theme means saying no to many groups who request time or who demand to lead workshops on their own topics.

Another challenge is maintaining quality by inviting excellent teachers, preachers, or presenters with proven experience instead of soliciting volunteers to lead or selecting teachers based on such things as which district they represent. The goal is to offer an event that people attend because they want to rather than because they have to, an occasion so excellent that people would attend even if there were no annual conference being held.

High-quality worship and preaching. Formerly, the Missouri Conference invited guest preachers and named a worship team to plan the principal worship services. Worship leaders, musicians, and liturgists for each service represented laity and clergy from across the conference. However, when we adopted our focus on congregational excellence, we changed tactics. We now select preachers from within our conference who have exhibited excellence in preaching and invite them to bring their own worship team. The team is accustomed to working together, they model excellence, and they give members the opportunity to learn how another congregation works. Preachers come from different size churches representing diverse worship styles, but all of them are selected for their excellence.

High-quality, relevant teaching. Every morning begins with a teaching session, usually led by an outside speaker or writer. In this regard, our tactics match those of most annual conferences. But we identified the teaching as a priority tactic for redefining annual conference, and we became more intentional about selecting speakers. We search for speakers who are so respected for their insights that people would attend even if there were no sessions. When possible, we contract with speakers far in advance and encourage people to read books they've written.

Best practices workshops. The annual conference provides twenty workshops. People can attend two workshops. Leaders are selected for their expertise, teaching ability, and outward focus. They also represent theological, ethnic, and gender diversity and a wide array of church contexts. Leaders are nominated by the cabinet, Mission Council, directors, and sessions team and then evaluated for quality and relevance. Most are pastors and laity from congregations within our conference, but some are writers, consultants, or church leaders from elsewhere. Workshop topics apply the annual conference theme to particular audiences, such as small churches, youth workers, Hispanic ministries, urban ministries, and so on. The only nonthematic workshops are those that focus on conference finances to provide time for questions on these topics.

Formerly, attendance at workshops was sporadic, and many people took the afternoon for free time. For the last several years, attendance has been overwhelming, with many nonconference members attending. Increasing the quality requires fighting the egalitarian notion that anyone who wants to can lead a workshop, whether or not it relates to the theme and regardless of the quality.

An outward focus. Another tactic is to create a deliberate focus on the mission field, reaching next generations, and serving our neighbors. Booths highlight mission opportunities, service projects, and the work of United Methodist agencies. Disaster response teams demonstrate equipment, and the Mozambique Initiative renews partnerships. Imagine No Malaria invites churches to give their Christmas offerings. Volunteers offer hands-on help with a local service project. The focus on congregational vitality serves the end of changing the world.

Increased youth leadership. It has been helpful to increase the number of youth serving as leaders at annual conference. At the Missouri Annual Conference, dozens of youth sit together on the front rows of sessions. Youth delegates are joined by several hundred youth from across the state for concerts, street parties, and work projects. Youth lead prayers and music, help with planning, and have preached at the ordination service. A strong youth presence fundamentally changes the tone of conference.

Fun and play. Pastors and laity need other ways to relate to one another in addition to business and worship. Some of the most formative and unifying moments that deepen affection and reinforce identity come through play. Play is a significant tactic in our strategy for redefining annual conference. Laughter, relaxation, spontaneity, and unstructured time sometimes do more to invigorate people for ministry than guest speakers and business reports. In recent years, annual conference attended a baseball game, enjoyed a street party, formed a line dance, watched a sand and shadow show, appreciated music and storytelling by the youth, and enjoyed African cuisines. "No banquets" is a mantra as the sessions team plans.

Minimized reporting. Nothing grinds down the spirit faster than an endless lineup of reports from committees, task forces, institutions, and officers. PowerPoint presentations and videos do little to stave off boredom. Reporting from the stage doesn't serve the conference's interests or the presenter's interests. It's better to take reports out of the agenda and to provide other channels for ministries to engage the conference, such as through booths, lunches, or apps.

Spiritual grounding. It's also important to ground annual conference in the Spirit. A spiritual formation team prepares online prayers for the days leading up to annual conference and weaves prayer and music into every session. Prayer partners staff a chapel where members go for respite and replenishment. A labyrinth is provided.

Explicit encouragement. One of the most important purposes of annual conference is to encourage. Pastors of various statuses are recognized and welcomed. Financial reports are replete with words of appreciation to churches for their giving. Young people are invited to consider full-time Christian ministry. Awards highlight victories for churches of all types. Teaching sessions are planned to edify rather than to arouse guilt or blame.

Radical hospitality. Annual conferences can revisit how they do hospitality. Legions of volunteers serve as greeters, ushers, and hosts. Every effort is made to streamline registration, provide excellent information, and anticipate needs. Volunteer teams help with traffic, doors, directions, and countless other amenities to exceed the expectations of participants.

Clarity of purpose. Without clarity of purpose, the participants lose focus. The bishop restates the fundamental purposes, priorities, and strategies of conference and then describes how the theme, speakers, and activities fit in the larger mission.

As voluntary as possible. Every effort is made to foster congregational self-determination. As part of this tactic, leaders consciously avoid words like *mandate, require, must, should,* and other coercive language. The Healthy Church Initiative, the Small Church Initiative, Pastoral Leadership Development groups, Lay Leadership Development groups, the Mozambique Initiative, Imagine No Malaria—all these are voluntary.

Continuing Challenges

The tactics sound familiar because most conferences have reconfigured annual conference sessions. The evolution is best seen by comparing an agenda for sessions today with an agenda from thirty years ago. Next generations will require more change. Even with redesign, the event still is perceived as having questionable relevance by younger attendees.

Many annual conferences are experimenting with shorter meetings, some set a day for learning apart from the business, and most send volunteers into the community for hands-on ministry while sessions are held.

A primary challenge all annual conferences face is expecting to conduct business with hundreds or thousands of participants while relying on the same processes a small governing board would use. The growing size of conference gatherings is an issue.

Annual conference sessions have grown in size as a result of the unintended consequences of numerous decisions. First, many conferences have merged with other conferences. Since every congregation receives at least one lay delegate, a merged conference has more delegates. Second, the *Book of Discipline* requires an equal number of lay delegates to clergy delegates. When General Conference added full-time and part-time local pastors to the deacons and elders to arrive at the clergy count, the equalization formula required that more laity be added. Third, including retired pastors in the equalization formula requires more laity to maintain the balance. Finally, General Conference regularly adds more district representatives or *ex-officio* members, such as district lay leaders, UMW and UMM leaders, and so forth.

The point isn't to argue the merits of any of these decisions; a good case could be made for each of these additions. However, the impact on size has been remarkable. In Missouri, which is a merged conference, the equalization formula requires that the 997 clergy in various categories be matched by 997 laity. Since many retirees, part-time local pastors, and lay members attend sporadically, attendance runs close to 1,600, plus several hundred spouses, guests, and staff. Including hosts, choirs, vendors, and others, we plan for two thousand people or more. That compares to gatherings of five hundred people forty years ago in the predecessor conferences, even though we now have three hundred fewer churches and eighty thousand fewer United Methodists in Missouri than we had back then.

Besides logistics and costs, the issue is the expectation that thorough business can be conducted using Robert's Rules, inviting anyone to question, amend, substitute, or debate every issue. Conferences that prepare months in advance, plan high-quality experiences, and streamline processes can get paralyzed by minutiae, stuck in trivialities, sabotaged by disgruntled people, or held hostage by a handful of members with special agendas.

Would you board a plane in which every passenger has a button marked "crash!" that can doom the plane?[6] Annual conference sessions sometimes feel like that—any one person can bring business to a halt and mire the whole body of people in endless debate. Anyone can amend, amend again, interrupt, change direction, ask for recounts, make referrals, lift points of order, and endlessly distract annual conference from its agenda and purpose.

What other organization do you belong to that holds meetings with two thousand people, utilizing the same rules and policies that one uses for a gathering of twenty?

A European company that markets electronic voting systems led a demonstration of its equipment for bishops. In Europe, publicly traded companies have no proxy system for shareholders, and so they hold large shareholder meetings that require electronic voting equipment. After the company developed the voting devices, they searched for other meetings with thousands of people that use legislative processes so that they could market their technology beyond Europe. According to the company representative, the only US organizations identified that have meetings of a thousand people or more with actual votes, ballots, amendments, and Robert's Rules are judicatories of mainline Protestant denominations! Other groups—legislatures, boards, directors, universities—use smaller governing entities, and large associations, such as political conventions and professional associations, vote up or down on recommendations from executive committees.

Large gatherings work wonderfully for reinforcing identity, unifying purpose, learning, and mobilizing people for the mission. And large gatherings work well for issues of low complexity and low conflict. But for issues of high complexity—health insurance plans, personnel policies, pension issues—an annual conference can unintentionally adopt amendments that contradict laws or leave the conference open to liability.

Especially for issues characterized by both high complexity and high conflict, an auditorium full of people doesn't work well. Many of us have been in sessions with people lining up at microphones, each wanting to edit the language of a different sentence in a two-page resolution on a highly controversial issue. Such issues, by their complexity, don't lend themselves to up or down votes, and there are as many competing claims, perspectives, and priorities as there are people in the room.

This doesn't mean we should disenfranchise anyone or deny members their rights of deliberation. But conferences must consider how to foster common purpose, transparency, and participation while deliberately protecting sessions from becoming bogged down, derailed, distracted, or sabotaged.

One basic tactic is to adopt standing rules that limit debate by agreeing to a small number of speeches and by limiting time allotted to each speaker. Most annual conferences do this already, knowing that the body can always suspend the rules to extend debate if necessary. Another tactic is to channel all work through existing committees that have been authorized and elected by the conference so that nothing can be introduced to the agenda from the floor without the required two-thirds vote to amend the agenda. Another tactic involves more thorough preparation and communication before and outside of annual conference sessions so that people have ample opportunity to express their opinions, suggest options, and have their questions addressed somewhere else besides on the floor of conference.

When conferences get sidetracked from their purpose, someone inevitably asks, "Why doesn't the bishop do something about this?" While a bishop shapes the vision through preaching and teaching, the bishop also must preside without being partial. The role of the presiding officer is to help the body do what it wills. Annual conferences that allow themselves to get mired in minutiae and torn by conflict are doing it to themselves. Whenever the majority has had enough, they can limit debate, close debate, table a motion, refer an action, or alter the agenda. The annual conference experience belongs to everyone, and we all own it. The conference has to take responsibility for its own behavior. We deserve the annual conferences we get.

A related challenge faced by annual conferences is the widespread use of resolutions and petitions to influence agendas. Many conferences receive dozens of resolutions from members or churches calling for the conference to send a letter to the governor, the president, or Congress expressing support or opposition to policies or to direct the work of another part of the church, such as a general board. Usually the issues are volatile, complex, and emotionally packed. Annual conferences can spend hours in heated arguments that divide the members or lose significant time amending resolutions to find enough common ground so that a modified version finally emerges with majority support. When annual conference planners solicit event evaluations, a majority of members describe resolutions as the most negative and unproductive aspect of the gathering.

Resolutions place annual conferences in a reactive rather than a proactive posture. Rather than ministries filtering through a process of planning, deliberation, and accountability, the annual conference responds to the agenda of a particular constituency.

An annual conference that gives large portions of time and energy to resolutions is practicing avoidance behavior. As painful as these debates may be, arguing about resolutions is easier than dealing with the church's failure to reach new people, young people, and more diverse people. Resolutions that require an up or down vote on controversial, complex issues are a demand for conformity in a denomination that values diverse perspectives. Such debate fosters a political environment rather than a learning, growing, exploring culture as people define themselves over against one another according to who is on whose side.

This isn't to suggest that United Methodists should avoid engagement with significant social or political issues or that we should cower from controversy or from issues about which we disagree. It's not the *what*, it's the *who* and the *how* that are problematic. The *what* is taking action related to our social principles or addressing unjust systems. The best *who* is the primary locus of our mission and our most influential point of contact with society, the local congregation; and the best *how* doesn't involve winning a vote of 51 percent at a conference.

The adoption of resolutions by an annual conference is one of the least effective ways of effecting change in society, and the strategy is based on outdated notions of the church's voice and its place in the larger culture. Adopting resolutions harkens back to a day when mainline denominations spoke with a powerful monolithic, monocultural voice to shape political will and to a time when a consensus from a denomination wielded influence. This is no longer the case.

A letter from an annual conference has little weight among the thousands of voices in the cultural mix today, and receiving a letter from a conference secretary announcing the adoption of a resolution by 53 percent means little to political leaders. A unified voice from a motivated congregation carries far more weight.

Resolutions change little or nothing out in the world, but they exact a great cost in broken community within the conference. Resolutions are recorded in the minutes, preserved in the journal, and remain there with little effect. They direct energy toward the center and toward changing one another, rather than toward changing the conditions of the world. Why try to force people into agreeing with us?

Many annual conferences have adopted methods for engaging controversial issues in a way so as not to disrupt other work. One tactic is giving the work back to congregations. Lift up congregations that exemplify positive engagement with an issue and invite other congregations to learn from them. Congregations teach other congregations. A second tactic is to set aside a place and time for meaningful, thoughtful dialogue on controversial issues in a forum that doesn't end with a vote. Invite trained moderators or experts on the topic. Emphasize learning, growing, understanding, listening, and action. People learn better when they aren't focused on who wins and who loses. A third tactic is to offer voluntary ways for people to get involved. Provide a table for people to sign a petition if they want to do so. A letter with several hundred signatures carries more weight than a divided annual conference vote. A fourth tactic involves adopting rules that limit the total amount of time allotted for resolutions and then only acting on those that are resolved during that time.

Reconfiguring Conference

The seventh lever, reconfiguring annual conference sessions, may seem the simplest, and yet it is critical. Just as Sunday worship is the most important hour of the week for congregations and deserves the highest and best attention by everyone involved, so the three days of annual conference are the most important to bring focus and purpose yearlong through the conference. Conference sessions lend critical support to all the other levers and strategies. Annual conference is the time to draw people into the mission and equip them to help.

Before we became more intentional about annual conference sessions, we had difficulty getting people to come for three days. Now our challenge is how to accommodate several hundred extra people who want to attend but who are not members. Actual business—reports, addresses, budgets, nominations, votes—has been reduced to about six hours. Annual conference has become a primary tool for supporting our larger mission.

Wesley's notes from the 1747 Conference record this discussion:

> Q: How may the time of this Conference be made more eminently a time of prayer, watching, and self-denial?
>
> A: 1. While we are in Conference, let us have an especial care to set God always before us. 2. In the intermediate hours, let us visit none but the sick, and spend all our time that remains in retirement, and 3. Let us then give ourselves unto prayer for one another, and for the blessing of God on this our labour.[7]

As people met with Mr. Wesley to "confer" together on their common ministry, he invited them to keep God front and center in their deliberations, to care for the poor and ill, and to pray for one another and for God's blessing on their work together. Every moment of the time together is infused with purpose. There are no meetings for the sake of meeting. All serve Christ.

Conference for John Wesley was an expression of the body of Christ, a visible sign of our connection to one another through Christ. Community in Christ is persevering and resilient and eternal, binding us to one another and tying us to those who have come before and those who will come after. And yet community in Christ is also fragile, something elegantly intangible and subtle, spiritual and breath-like; it requires of us great intentionality and care. The threads of grace that bind us to Christ and to one another require sustained and gentle attention by all of us. Perhaps this is what John Wesley meant by, "Let us have *an especial care* to set God always before us" when he invites us to focus on the mission of Christ and to pray for one another through all the organizational deliberations. Our mission begins in Christ and ends in Christ.

Conversation Questions

What would you say is the most important purpose of gathering annually for conference? Learning, worship, fellowship, information, business, participation, affirmation, inspiration—what do you most hope to receive from your time at annual conference?

How has "conferring" together in the Wesleyan way strengthened your ministry? How do your conference sessions expand ministry, encourage spiritual growth, and extend the United Methodist witness, and how does it limit or discourage ministry?

How well do conference sessions reinforce a sense of common identity and purpose?

What frustrates you the most about conference sessions, and why? What feeds you and inspires you? How would you reshape the annual conference agenda?

How do you remain passionately engaged with those who view things differently from you?

What changes would help your annual conference conduct business with greater transparency, thoroughness, and participation while also operating more efficiently in a large gathering?

INNOVATION AND IMAGINATION

Good strategies are generally so simple and straightforward as to appear self-evident, and yet if they remain unidentified or unarticulated, they fail to draw the focus of the conference's work on what matters most. And as Lawrence Bassidy, former CEO of Allied Signal suggests, strategies are intellectually simple; their execution is not.[1]

Putting strategies into practice is extraordinarily difficult, and it is never merely the result of a single person's decision, the recommendation of a team, or the vote of a conference. Strategies, and the tactics that support them, are crafted day-by-day, step-by-step, meeting-by-meeting, person-by-person as leaders commit resources to initiatives aligned with the mission. Execution involves interweaving strategy with reality, an approach toward getting things done that fits the context. Strategies may start simple, but they become more comprehensive as others from throughout the conference get involved.

A well-defined set of strategies, simply articulated and widely pursued, changes a conference. Strategies provide the channels for purposeful work. A stream without banks has neither direction nor movement. Any major activity that isn't moving an organization toward its mission is likely moving it away from it.

Strategies are difficult to execute because they require changing operational systems. Conference leaders can't direct resources in strategic ways without taking on leadership tasks rather than mere management tasks. Rather than keeping the machinery going smoothly, leaders make hard decisions, against predictable resistance, to focus on the mission.

"Culture eats strategy for breakfast every day," Peter Drucker reportedly said,[2] underlining the difficulty of executing strategies in a system that prefers equilibrium rather than interruption. But culture is simply behaviors, attitudes, and values. Culture is formed by sustained strategies. Obedience to a clear mission with defined strategies changes culture.

The Seven Levers are meant to stimulate fresh thinking rather than to offer the final word. This is no attempt to standardize operations across conferences. Standardization forces conferences to adopt systems that don't match the context and the mission field. Every conference has to arrive at its own strategies.

Other Levers

These seven aren't the only levers available to conferences. A lever is any strategy that leaders use to derive disproportionate results for the mission relative to the amount of work applied. A particular context may make it essential to give priority to other levers. Some other levers might include:

A strategy for setting large churches free. Large, growing, healthy churches are essential to the future of our mission, yet they often feel out of sync, neglected, or restrained by the conference. Large churches do an excellent job of developing staff and can provide future leaders. They shouldn't be constrained from recruiting talented staff. Gifted seminarians or candidates may not be attracted to a conference in general but would be thrilled at the prospect of working on a dynamic staff. Furthermore, large congregations have the organizational capacity and the vision to start churches or second sites. They should be encouraged and resourced rather than criticized and controlled. Large churches can lead mission initiatives that draw other congregations into participation. They can become teaching congregations. It's imperative that conferences work with large churches to multiply their positive impact rather than burden them with irrelevant tasks and unnecessary restraints. A strategy for setting large churches free is one of the best levers that conference leaders have.

A strategy for empowering gifted, young pastors. If the only statistic we could fully comprehend about The United Methodist Church in the United States is that our median age is approaching sixty, while the median age of our culture is thirty-five, we would see with stark clarity the missional challenge we face. There is an age gap of nearly two generations between the average United Methodist and the local mission field. Across that gap lie significant differences in perception, spirituality, musical tastes, community, life experience, use of technology, and cultural value. While pastors of all ages are needed to fulfill our mission, reaching next generations requires gifted young people.

A strategy for empowering gifted young pastors involves the bishop and other leaders protecting the voice of young adults and inviting them into leadership on their own terms instead of expecting them to do things the way we have done them. A strategy involves reverse mentoring, in which older pastors learn from younger ones about how to reach next generations. It may involve entrusting larger appointments to fruitful pastors at an earlier age in situations where the demographics of the mission field indicate it and supporting expressions of ministry outside the ordination track. Engaging younger pastors isn't about asking them to serve on committees but about fostering openness and innovation. Let them lead.

A strategy for quality lay-leadership development. This strategy includes tactics such as training and support for at least three types of laypersons: those who want to learn how to lead their current congregations better; those willing to teach and preach in other congregations; and those feeling called to serve in a pastoral role as lay ministers. All three groups include people with a vision for ministry and capacities for service larger than their own congregations. The recent changes in nomenclature in the *Book of Discipline* regarding lay servants, lay speakers, and certified lay ministers may have confused rather than clarified these distinct callings. A conference strategy must begin with the end in mind, refuse to compromise on quality, and provide opportunities for lay development. Inviting laity to lead and use their creativity is an underutilized lever.

A better strategy for closing churches. Conferences, like all organizations, must decide when it's right to pull back on, shut down, or abandon ministries that once served a purpose fruitfully and do so no longer. Congregations follow a life cycle. Every church closes. None of the churches Paul counseled in his letters still exist, not because they failed but because they prospered, fulfilled their purpose, and eventually faded from view as other churches carried on the mission.

Without a strategy, churches deplete their resources, their buildings deteriorate until they become liabilities, fewer people are left to make good decisions, and nothing remains to carry on the mission for future generations. With a strategy, superintendents engage churches earlier that exhibit indicators of irreversible decline, discuss alternatives, and help congregations make better decisions about property before they become liabilities.

A humane strategy for removing ineffective clergy. Three to 5 percent of clergy are ineffective and are unable or unwilling to learn the skills for healthy leadership. The same percentage applies to nearly all professions. The *Discipline* provides supervisory processes, but the nonlinear language is confusing, requires referring to numerous paragraphs that seem contradictory, and is useless unless conferences are willing to follow through when a case merits it. A strategy for addressing clergy ineffectiveness includes bringing together the cabinet and Board of Ordained Ministry to adopt a clear linear statement of the process, including supervisory conversations, evaluations, expectations, timelines, plans for improvement, fair process, and consequences. The policy relies upon the *Discipline*'s components but outlines them in an understandable way. Another tactic involves training counselors to talk to pastors about alternatives, such as retirement, other careers, and so on. Conferences are changing the language of exiting or intervention policy to adopt a more supportive posture that encourages exploring a call to different paths, such as Indiana Conference's *Called Anew-Sent with Love*. Another tactic is offering financial resources to bridge concerns about health insurance or transition costs.

An Environment of Innovation

The Seven Levers represent insight gleaned from the experiments of many conferences. This time of flux and fluidity requires innovation, exploration, and permission to try new approaches.

Sometimes we're so keenly aware of how "methodized" we are, with our rules, policies, structures, and disciplines, that we overlook the bold originality that characterized John Wesley and the early Methodists. Methodism began as a wildly creative experiment, risky and countercultural. Wesley's notions of forming classes, bands, and societies; of founding preaching houses and schools; of inner holiness and outward witness; of mobilizing people to visit the imprisoned and feed the poor; of field preaching and ordaining pastors for America—these experiments derived from an expansive and adventuresome sense of God's grace. Early Methodism was outward focused and future oriented, innovative and energetic.

In a similar spirit, leaders today must evolve from "What shall we do?" to "What shall we try?" and "What do we need to learn?" For this era, there are no experts, only practitioners. We have to encourage bold experimentations and learn from each other.

Marissa Mayer, when she served as vice president at Google, outlined *Nine Principles of Innovation*, and several of these are relevant to our task.[3]

First, she suggests *ideas come from everywhere*. Ideas come from the top and also from the bottom, from the center and from the margins, from laity as well as pastors, from other conferences and from our own congregations, from other denominations as well as corporations. Expect people to have ideas, and provide systems so that people can contribute ideas, sort through them, and experiment. People need permission to try things— launch ministries, start churches, reach new communities, serve unmet needs.

Second, Mayer says *work with gifted people*. Convening conversations with highly talented clergy and laity and drawing high-performing leaders into the task of addressing key challenges accelerates innovation. Gifted people are focused on the cutting edge, constantly learning, given to experimentation, and asking for more opportunity. They are proactive. How can we learn from them?

Mayer's third principle of innovation is *share everything you can*. In a flat organization, learning and leadership don't come from the top. Pastors learn from pastors, laypersons learn from laity, churches learn from other churches. In an open culture, new ideas and best practices spread through networks with a minimum of territoriality. The attitude of every conference can be "Step into our workshop, ask anything you want, borrow what you like, and tell us how you do things so that we can learn from you, too." If a congregation discovers an approach that works, give them the forum to teach others. Give away as much as possible.

Fourth, Marissa Mayer suggests that leaders *give people license to pursue their dreams*. Rather than expecting everyone to use the template of "This is how we always do it," give them permission to use their passions and creativity to explore new ways. Cabinets and staff need to feel the freedom, and give the permission, to try bold new things without fear of failure.

"Can we think about a second site? Can we talk with a declining church about repurposing the building? Can we launch our own college-age ministry? Can we initiate a relationship with Sudan? Can we experiment with house churches?" Just say Yes. Set leaders free.

Fifth, Mayer reminds us that *innovation doesn't mean instant perfection*. Experiments by their very definition don't always turn out as planned. Some initiatives never find traction, and some plans change so radically that they take a form no one ever anticipated. Innovation requires feedback that allows for quick adjustments, and the best projects require little corrections every day. Without failure-tolerant conference leaders, pastors and laity won't feel free to experiment.

The sixth principle, *data is apolitical*, may not seem directly relevant, but it is. Innovative organizations can't avoid the numbers and must drill down to determine what works and what doesn't. Programs can't continue because of politics—to protect a pet project or a supervisor's favorite worker. Base decisions on data.

The seventh principle is that *creativity loves constraints*. Every project works within limits set by money, time, people, and context. Working our way through to fruitful ministries requires extraordinary creativity. Limits set by a defined mission sharpen clarity and focus resources. Christ turned a few loaves into nourishment for thousands and God took a handful of ordinary disciples and changed the world. Christians have a long history of working within constraints.

In Marissa Mayer's world of technology, the eighth principle is simply *users, users, users*, calling innovators to put the experience of the customer first. In our context, the principle might be *mission field, mission field, mission field*. Innovation requires constant attention to those God has entrusted us to serve. Innovation demands an outward focus, a missional purpose.

The ninth principle is, *don't kill projects, morph them*. When a good idea has momentum but isn't working to the potential intended, repurpose the project to make it work.

What are the best decisions you ever made as a leader? What are the best decisions your conference ever made? To try something? To risk something? To initiate something? These are decisions to experiment. An environment of innovation is imperative.

Imagine becoming the conference that figures out a better way of connecting with urban youth whom our current congregations have trouble reaching or becoming the conference that discovers a way to repopulate rural areas with United Methodist house churches. Imagine becoming the conference that develops a way to start sustainable congregations that reach the working poor. Imagine becoming the conference that explores a new framework for funding that doesn't depend upon an apportionment system. Solutions to these and other challenges can only be explored through experimentation within a culture of innovation.

The Adjacent Possible

Innovative solutions don't spring forth in a final form that's fit for every context. Change seldom follows a consistent trend in one direction, and a single moment of inspiration seldom propels us toward a perfect solution. Instead, innovative thinking is a slow and gradual process, full of fits and starts, progress and setbacks, projects that succeed wonderfully and others that fail spectacularly.

Why didn't Alexander Graham Bell invent the cellular phone in the 1870s instead of the landline? Hundreds of thousands of miles of copper wiring and millions of telephone posts could have been saved if he'd simply started with mobile devices rather than bulky black box phones.

The answer is obvious. None of the technologies were yet available to take such a leap. His work on the wired phone had to come first, followed by decades of improvement and refinement, the discoveries of radio waves and nanotechnologies, the making of plastics and microprocessors, and so forth. The adjacent technologies didn't exist, the science was not ready, and the foundations hadn't been laid.

In his book, *Where Good Ideas Come From*, Steven Johnson advances the idea of "The Adjacent Possible."[4] Usually what we create through our current innovations isn't the ultimate solution but only the opening for later solutions. Innovation breaks down existing structures to allow someone else to figure things out. Experimentation often doesn't solve a problem; rather it moves us out of the place we are stuck so that someone else can solve it.

The adjacent possible is the available next step in innovation. It's the possible combinations that now exist because of multiple innovations. Sometimes we know where we want to go, but all we can do is open the door to the next room. Experimentation has us leaving one room for another. We move forward to where we want to go one room at a time.

The adjacent possible is the next room, the set of opportunities at the boundaries of our reach. The boundaries move as we explore them. Each new room brings more doors to try. Each time we take a different approach toward ministry, it opens doors for us and others and causes us to see things differently than before.

Experiments with college-age ministries in Missouri may increase our capacity to reach dozens of new young people. But our experiments may not take us to a fully satisfactory solution. And yet our innovations may open the doors for people in other conferences to think differently about their campus ministries, and it may give them courage to experiment on their own. Other experiments when combined with our own may help us discover a model that reaches tens of thousands of young people we would never have reached with outdated and unfruitful models. What we discover isn't the final answer, but it may lead to an adjacent possible, a model we can't now see. We may be building something akin to Alexander Graham Bell's big boxy black phone so that someone someday can develop a model with many times the capacity.

Experiments by conferences with different models for starting new churches, designing sustainable ministry with the poor, supporting non-traditional expressions of ministry, or reinventing financial systems—these help us all move forward, so long as we are connecting with each other and communicating ideas instead of protecting them. We can't afford systems that limit, punish, or restrict exploration. A culture of innovation requires active sharing, learning, and teaching. We need to be willing to share our failures as well as our successes. Part of our gift to others is sharing what we learn from what goes wrong.

The point of sharing isn't to see who wins, who comes in first, or who impresses everyone else. Comparison kills creativity. On the other hand, curiosity feeds learning and moves us forward. What we have to learn as a denomination, no one can teach us. We will learn it by working together in a culture of bold, missional experimentation.

More and more conferences are working on prototypes. They are deconstructing then reconstructing. They are leaving one room for another, thereby opening doors for others to follow. Some of these experiments shatter existing assumptions. For instance, when you think *congregation,* or *district,* or *superintendent*, what comes to mind? Within thirty years, the fundamental form of each of these will be radically different from today. In fact, they may have to take a different form for us to remain faithful to our mission.

Wesley could not have made field preaching thrive without the countercultural work of George Whitefield. Wesley's experiment with small groups when he was a student at Oxford helped him perfect the class meetings that later resourced Methodism's extraordinary growth. A simple gathering in 1744, and the salutary effect it had on Methodist leaders, caused Wesley to repeat it until it formed into a conference, an extraordinary tool for multiplying ministry. One thing builds on another. That's the adjacent possible.

Are we bold enough to experiment with the forms we've inherited in order to further the mission of Christ? Are we creative enough and confident enough to allow old and unnecessary systems to fall away?

Reframing Critical Conversations

A culture of innovation and experimentation requires reframing critical conversations.[5] Conferences become trapped repeating the same conversations, holding the same debates, and locked up in the same conflict. Every conference has its long-standing points of contention. Can we reframe issues in missional terms rather than replaying the old tapes that divide us along traditional lines?

For instance, every conference struggles with budgets, apportionments, rising costs, and lower-income streams. This inevitably leads to technical conversations about raising money or changing the apportionment formula. Perhaps we need to change the question from, "How do we raise more money?" to "In the next phase of Wesleyan Methodism, what's the center that holds us together and multiplies our missional effectiveness, and what are the costs?" Reframing the question interrupts the technical approach and moves toward a deeper question about the future forms of connectionalism.

Every conference struggles to cover the costs of their legacy commitments, the historic obligations that are annually reflected in the budget, even though no conference would undertake such costs anew if starting conference from scratch. Instead of the questions, "How can we afford our conference camps?" or, "Do we sell them or raise huge amounts of money to improve them?," perhaps the questions should be, "How do we foster spiritual formation for children in an era when young people don't seem to have time for camping or when they want better facilities than what we can offer?" and "Is there a conference role for strengthening the spiritual formation of children, or does that task belong to congregations?"

Every conference is rethinking the effectiveness of their campus ministries, but they approach the topic with questions such as, "Are our campus ministries fruitful or not? How do we fund them? How do we evaluate them?" Perhaps a better question is, "How do we best shape Christian formation for young adults, and what are the platforms and models worth exploring and supporting?" Traditional conversations get stuck in an up-or-down, yes-or-no polarity about funding a single model for reaching college-age young adults when there are dozens of models that deserve consideration.

Another example of reframing the question focuses on the role of the general church in relationship to conferences and congregations. The primary technical questions are, "How do we lower general church costs?" or "How can we restructure general church governance?" Another approach might ask, "In a flat world in which conferences and congregations can do more things for themselves and vertical structures no longer serve well, what is the center of a new connectionalism?" or "How do we convert structures of control to structures of empowerment, and what would a simpler and more permission-giving experiment look like?" or "If connectionalism in its current form is demanding too much uniformity, how can we 'subvert' the restraining aspects of our bureaucracy to foster fresh expressions of ministry?"

When conference takes on responsibilities and ministries that more appropriately belong to congregations, it weakens congregations and dulls their witness. Conferences that do ministry *instead of* or *on behalf of* congregations, remove churches from the front lines of engagement with the communities they serve. It may help to reframe the question from "How does the conference develop more ministries with the poor, that relieve suffering, confront injustice, and further the Methodist witness?" to "How can the conference increase the number of congregations that serve the poor, relieve suffering, confront injustice, and further the Methodist witness?"

From Events to Processes

A culture of innovation requires moving from events that focus on change to actually experimenting with new systems that are more conducive to our mission. In recent years, the majority of US conferences have invited guest speakers to conference sessions, clergy retreats, lay gatherings, and planning meetings to address the need for change. This is a good sign, and it should continue. Interest in such events reveals a yearning for new approaches. People are ready for change. Workshops and presentations deepen the conversation and motivate leaders.

But *processes* rather than *events* are the key. Guest speakers inspire and consultants teach, but processes move us forward. Conferences can't change merely as a result of hosting sequences of events. At some point, people need to sit down and work through complex tasks of reinventing the systems by which they operate.

Operational change may start small. The most important tactics that sustain the Missouri Conference strategies—the Healthy Church Initiative, Pastoral Leadership Development groups, systems for starting new churches and recruiting clergy—were never put before conference for vote, and they haven't required policy changes. These projects began with teams given the freedom to experiment. Eventually, with continued refinement, these programs gained wider participation, and we adapted our processes accordingly.

Operational change addresses processes, such as who, what, where, when, how much, timeframes, benchmarks, communication, evaluation, and progress toward goals. We will never get there by talking about the need to turn churches around; eventually someone has to actually experiment with an intervention system.

Conversation Questions

How clear are you about the fundamental strategies that drive your conference? Would others identify the same strategies as you? How well does your conference do at identifying strategies and developing operations to support them?

How would your conference change if it committed to performing these seven strategies with excellence? What excites you about that? What scares you?

What other levers come to mind that could inordinately influence positive change in your conference?

How does your conference foster an atmosphere of innovation and experimentation? How do you receive and give permission to try new things? How do new ideas emerge from various sources, and how are they received and developed?

What's an experimental approach your conference has tried that other conferences could learn from? What have you tried and failed that others might learn from?

How does the idea of the adjacent possible offer affirmation to you about the benefits of experimentation and innovation? What ministries, initiatives, and experiments give you hope?

How might a conference operate differently if it focused more on young people? What would a church look like that goes where young people go and cares about what young people care about?

What critical issues does your conference face that may require a reframing of the question in order to break through to innovative solutions?

How does your conference learn to do things differently? What's the most risky, bold, and innovative experiment your conference has tried?

Epilogue

The Seven Levers provide a language to help leaders articulate strategies so that conferences can begin to work on processes and systems. Of the fifty-seven US conferences, at least ten are boldly experimenting with one or several of these strategies, and they are showing good outcomes. None of us have this all down pat.

A half-dozen or more conferences are overtly refusing to experiment because of clergy resistance, protection of prerogative, unmitigated conflict, denial and avoidance, rigidity for the old ways, or a lack of critical leadership. These regions are unable or unwilling to try anything substantially different.

Between these two extremes are dozens of conferences, the majority of our church, who desire change, yearn for new approaches, and want to do something different but aren't sure what change looks like or how to get there. These conferences are curious, interested, and eager, and they value the conversation. These are the conferences ready to move from events to processes.

Imagine a day when conferences more intentionally collaborate with one another, teaching and learning, sharing experiments, and working together on joint projects.

Imagine networks of churches starting new churches across conference boundaries, using the resources and expertise from one area of the connection to stimulate greater fruitfulness in another area.

Imagine conferences unable to afford staff that are pooling resources with other conferences to share specialized leadership.

Imagine congregational intervention systems operating across conference boundaries by invitation so that conferences learn from conferences.

Imagine cabinets from several conferences convening to learn from one another about appointment processes and strategies for cultivating clergy excellence.

Imagine bishops gathering to work through case studies, to process challenges together, to collaborate on critical appointments, and to sharpen their leadership skills.

Imagine executive teams comprised of conference leaders meeting with teams from other conferences to evaluate their own governance systems and to suggest ways of streamlining and aligning resources.

Imagine developing an intervention process for conferences, much like the Healthy Church Initiative or similar to a university ten-year review, that invites an objective trained team of outside consultants or colleagues to evaluate systems and to offer recommendations for change.

These conversations and collaborations are already happening in various parts of our connection. How can we make such learning more intentional? How can your conference join in?

The future of all of our conferences depends upon our ability to learn from one another. Conferences that collaborate and learn together are connected by their common mission, a more compelling, relevant, and effective expression of connectionalism than mere structural connectionalism.

Seven Choices

Investing time in strategies and tactics can sound boring, mundane, laborious. Where's the spirit, spontaneity, and excitement that comes with ministry? But a focus on the inner workings is not inconsistent with a passion for reaching out, and time given to strategy can foster extraordinary creativity. As we see in Wesley and our forbearers, leaders can be strategic and creative, tactical and pioneering, disciplined and innovative, detailed and intuitive. Conferences can attend to improving their inner processes while focusing outward to the mission field. In fact, if we fail to address strategies and tactics, we will continue to grow weaker, less relevant, and less engaged with the mission of Christ. The Seven Levers provide a path to relevance and fruitfulness.

These levers represent seven choices that will drive our future.

Will we get better, more consistent, and more innovative with starting congregations, or will we neglect our best tool for reaching next generations?

Will we commit to the practice of quality clergy peer learning for support and skill enhancement or continue to blame seminaries for poor preparation?

Will we develop effective intervention systems for churches that request them or allow the majority of our congregations to slowly age and decline?

Will we make hard decisions about clergy fruitfulness and accountability or avoid decisions and deny that there is a problem?

Will we streamline governance systems to invigorate the mission of the church, or will we struggle with confusing and ineffective committees?

Will we align our resources to multiply our missional impact or continue to allow them to be so widely dispersed that they accomplish none of the most critical tasks a conference must perform?

Will we reclaim the purpose of annual conference sessions so that they cultivate a culture of learning and a missional identity, or will we allow them to degenerate into mere business sessions marked by conflict and bound by rules?

The Seven Levers provide a place for everyone to catch hold and do their part. These strategies provide a role for lay leaders, superintendents, conference staff, and the various boards and teams that govern a conference. Work can start with pastors or laity or congregations. From whatever your vantage point, there's a way to get involved, to contribute, to encourage, to lead.

Each lever feeds the others, and progress in a few areas fosters interest on other fronts. Just as painting a wall in a home makes us more acutely aware of other walls that need painting, and then of fixtures that need replacing and of floors that need retiling, successful progress with one lever stimulates the desire to address others. A conference doesn't have to begin at all places at once, and nearly all conferences are already doing something related to each lever. Explicitly naming a strategy or calling it a lever increases intentionality. Efforts coalesce, and work begins.

A Future with Hope

United Methodism's theology of grace, varieties of worship, emphasis on inner holiness and social witness, global vision, hymnody, our ability to hold together head and heart, our respect for women and men, our openness to people of all nations and ethnicities, our vision to transform the world through audacious projects like Imagine No Malaria—these form an expression of Christianity, a way of following Jesus, that can reach people that no other faith expression is able to reach. We offer a *both/and* theology in an *either/or* world. I'm not saying our approach is better than all the others; I'm merely suggesting that people who can't respond to other expressions can respond to the truth of Christ through our expression of faith. This form of faith and practice reached me, and without The United Methodist Church I suspect I would never have become a Christian.

The goal of rethinking our practices and revitalizing our churches isn't to save the denomination or the institutions of the church. Those who accuse people involved in leading change of merely working for institutional survival are misinformed or misunderstand. The reason I pour myself into the ministry and into leading the church comes from a deep-rooted place inside. It is grounded in the grace I have experienced, an initiating love that sought and found me through countless people who brought me God's unconditional love. This desire to share God's grace is God-given and sacred.

Methodism began as a way of life, and this way of life, deep-rooted in our theology and practice, is worthy of fostering, not for our sake but for the love of God in Christ.

Conferences are an incredible and unique tool derived from our earliest Methodist roots, an instrument for multiplying ministries and going places to reach people no one else can reach. Conferences are the Methodist advantage, a means for multiplying ministry other denominations don't have. But United Methodists are frustrated with our structure. They love their congregations, embrace our theology, and desire to change the world while also finding our structure increasingly less relevant and effective. Our excessive control and focus on rules becomes a stumbling block, causing us to focus our energies on ourselves rather than outward. Do we merely repeat and deepen the polity of Wesley and the early Methodists, adding more complexity to an already dense and inflexible structure? Or do we repeat the creativity, boldness, courage, and passion of our forbearers?

In another time of flux and fluidity in the church, John Wesley wrote the Covenant Prayer. Especially when we pray it near the New Year, sometimes we view the words as aspiration, as full of resolve. We pray it aloud together with the energy of repeating the pledge of allegiance, with an air of triumph or determination rather than humility.

This way of praying the Covenant Prayer misses the utterly intense vulnerability in the words. The prayer is a confession that we aren't in control,

167

we don't know what's next, and so we surrender ourselves in complete humility to God. The prayer isn't for when we are riding high and full of confidence but when we are feeling helpless and unsure. The Covenant Prayer is for those who don't have all the answers. Despite our brokenness, failure, and confusion, the prayer reminds us that there is a direction, a purpose and mission large and grand enough to submit our lives to.

The Covenant Prayer invites complete humility and obedience to God, asking God to work *through* us or to work *around* us, and to take us to places and to put us alongside people we would never choose if left to our own inclinations. Repeating the prayer in humility, we rededicate ourselves to Christ and reaffirm our willingness to adapt our lives to the mission field.

> I am no longer my own, but thine.
> Put me to what thou wilt, rank me with whom thou wilt.
> Put me to doing, put me to suffering.
> Let me be employed by thee or laid aside by thee,
> exalted for thee or brought low for thee.
> Let me be full, let me be empty.
> Let me have all things, let me have nothing.
> I freely and heartily yield all things
> to thy pleasure and disposal.[1]

Pray the Covenant Prayer together. Change the singular pronouns to plural so we speak as a community, so that it's about a whole conference, committee, or team. Let us offer ourselves up afresh to God, confessing our complete vulnerability and humility.

We might ask why anyone would pour themselves into the work of leading a conference today. Why would pastors and lay leaders give time to these strategies rather than focus on their local church? Are we serving on conference teams and task forces to help the church die with dignity or because we have nothing better to do with our time? God forbid. May we instead offer ourselves in leadership because we believe that The United Methodist Church has a vital witness to offer and that conferences provide an extraordinary means to multiply ministry, mobilize disciples, and reach people with the good news that God has met our highest hopes and deepest needs in Jesus Christ.

Conversation Questions

What elements of our faith and practice form a way of following Christ that made The United Methodist Church the way for God to reach you?

What are some of the habits, values, and attitudes that need to change in order for your conference to thrive in its mission? How willing are you to change your habits, values, and attitudes in order for the conference to thrive?

Have you ever voluntarily stepped down or stepped aside so that a ministry could move in a new direction? Where did the spiritual discernment come from to help you do this?

When was a time you experienced God working around you rather than through you? How did it feel?

Where do you see signs of a new church, of a burgeoning of life through fruitful ministry?

What initiatives and ministries in your conference or congregation give you hope?

What makes it worth the effort to strengthen United Methodist witness?

How do you personally feed the passion for ministry while also fostering the patience to work through an organization that responds slowly?

NOTES

The Complexity of Conferences

1. Lovett H. Weems Jr., *Focus: The Real Challenges that Face The United Methodist Church* (Nashville: Abingdon Press, 2011), 77.

2. Bryce G. Hoffman, *An American Icon: Alan Mulally and the Fight to Save Ford Motor Company* (New York: Crown Business, 2012), 120–24.

3. Ibid., 122.

4. The original 248 page Towers Watson Report can be read or downloaded at http://www.umccalltoaction.org/wp-content/uploads/challenge/CTA_STEERING%20 TEAM_%20RPT_1-44.pdf or by searching Towers Watson Steering Team Report 2010.

5. Ibid., 20–23.

Why Working Harder Isn't Helping

1. Thomas L. Friedman, *The World is Flat: A Brief History of the Twenty-First Century* (New York: Farrar, Straus, and Giroux, 2005).

2. Gordon MacKenzie, *Orbiting the Giant Hairball: A Corporate Fool's Guide to Surviving with Grace* (New York: Viking Penguin, 1998).

3. Adapted from MacKenzie, 39.

4. For a good description of "the power of no" in an organization, see Gil Rendle, *Back To Zero: The Search to Rediscover the Methodist Movement* (Nashville: TN: Abingdon Press, 2011), 74–76.

5. Jim Collins, *Good to Great and the Social Sector: A Monograph to Accompany Good to Great* (Boulder, CO: Jim Collins, 2005).

6. Ibid., 10.

7. Ibid., 1.

8. David Kinnaman and Gabe Lyons, *UnChristian: What a New Generation Really Thinks about Christianity, and Why It Matters* (Grand Rapids, MI: Baker Books, 2007), 28–29.

Finding Focus

1. Jim Collins, *Good to Great and the Social Sector: A Monograph to Accompany Good to Great* (Boulder, CO: Jim Collins, 2005), 1.

2. John P. Kotter, "Accelerate!," in *Harvard Business Review*, November 2012, 44–58.

3. John P. Kotter, *Leading Change* (Boston, MA: Harvard Business Review Press, 2012), 53–68.

4. Ronald A. Heifetz and Marty Linsky, *Leadership on the Line: Staying Alive through the Dangers of Leading* (Boston, MA: Harvard School of Business, 2002), 41.

5. *The Book of Discipline of The United Methodist Church* (Nashville: The United Methodist Publishing House, 2012), paragraph 120.

The First Lever:
A Strategy for Starting New Churches

1. For an excellent discussion about the impact of new churches, see chapter 2 of Stephen Compton's *Rekindling the Mainline: New Life through New Churches* (Bethesda, MD: The Alban Institute, 2003).

2. For a helpful approach to church mergers that avoids the worst pitfalls, see Jim Tomberlin and Warren Bird, *Better Together: Making Church Mergers Work* (San Francisco: Jossey-Bass, 2012).

The Second Lever:
A Strategy for Clergy Peer Learning

1. *Is the Treatment the Cure? A Study of the Effects of Participation in Pastoral Leadership Groups*, conducted through Austin Presbyterian Seminary, April 2010. For the complete study, search "Is the Treatment the Cure?" or download at http://www.samford.edu/uploaded Files/RCPE/Content/Is%20the%20Treatment%20the%20Cure.pdf.

2. Ibid, 10.

3. Dietrich Bonhoeffer, *Life Together: A Discussion of Christian Fellowship*, trans. John W. Doberstein (New York: Harper and Row, 1954), 20.

4. Paul D. Borden, *Hit the Bullseye: How Denominations Can Aim Congregations at the Mission Field* (Nashville: Abingdon Press, 2003).

5. For a good discussion on proximate outcomes, see Gil Rendle's monograph, *Convening a New Conversation*, a resource from the Texas Methodist Foundation, 2012, 17–18. The essay can be found by searching the title or at http://www.tmfinstitute.org/documents/Questions_Dev_of_Clergy_Leaders.pdf on the TMF Institute website.

The Third Lever:
A Strategy for Congregational Intervention

1. Robert Schnase, *Five Practices of Fruitful Congregations* (Nashville: Abingdon Press, 2007).

The Fourth Lever:
A Strategy for Cultivating Clergy Excellence

1. *A Lewis Center Report on Changes in Congregations, Clergy, and Deployment—2002–2012—Missouri Conference.* The report was commissioned by the South Central Jurisdiction for each of the conferences in the jurisdiction and completed in May 2013, by the Lewis Center for Church Leadership, Wesley Theological Seminary, Washington, DC.

2. Gil Rendle, *Back to Zero: The Search to Rediscover the Methodist Movement* (Nashville, TN: Abingdon Press, 2011), 36.

3. Lovett Weems and Tom Berlin, *Bearing Fruit: Ministry with Real Results* (Nashville: Abingdon Press, 2011); see chapter 3.

4. The questions for those called to preach go through several permutations and refinements from 1746 to 1756. For one early set, see Albert Outler, *John Wesley* (New York: Oxford University Press, 1964), 160–61.

5. For a more thorough discussion of the ecosystem metaphor for cultivating clergy leadership, see Bishop Janice Huie's monograph, "A New Paradigm for Clergy Leadership: Cultivating an Ecosystem of Excellence" by searching for the title or by downloading http://www.tmf-fdn.org/documents/monographs2013/9.3.13EcosystemofExcellence_Layout_1.pdf

The Fifth Lever:
A Strategy for Aligning Budgets and Resources

1. Kennon L Callahan, *Twelve Keys to an Effective Church: Strategic Planning for Mission* (San Francisco: Harper and Row, 1983), xiv.

2. *The Book of Discipline of The United Methodist Church* (Nashville: The United Methodist Publishing House, 2012), paragaph 336.

The Sixth Lever:
A Strategy for Creating Technically Elegant
Governance Systems

1. "Important Lessons from Peter Drucker" in *Netfax*, July 7, 1997, a newsletter from Leadership Network, Tyler, TX.

2. John Wigger, *American Saint: Francis Asbury and the Methodists* (New York: Oxford University Press, 2009), 9.

3. The words "technically elegant" to describe the goal of organizational alignment are from Franklyn Covey Company's *The 4 Roles of Leadership*, a seminar for leaders, 1999.

The Seventh Lever:
A Strategy for Reconfiguring Conference Sessions

1. Albert Outler, *John Wesley* (New York: Oxford University Press, 1964), 134.

2. *John Wesley, the Methodist by a Methodist Preacher* (New York: Methodist Book Concern, 1903); see chapter 13. Accessed on wesley.nnu.edu, 2012.

3. Russell E. Richey, *The Methodist Conference in America: A History* (Nashville: Kingswood Books, 1996).

4. Patrick Lencioni, *The Advantage: Why Organizational Health Trumps Everything Else in Business* (San Francisco: Jossey-Bass, 2012), 77–78.

5. Robert Schnase, *Remember the Future: Praying for the Church and Change* (Nashville: Abingdon Press, 2012).

6. This metaphor has been used by Bill Joy of Sun Microsystems in presentations about the future of technology.

7. Outler, *John Wesley*, 164.

Innovation and Imagination

1. Larry Bossidy and Ram Charan, *Execution: The Discipline of Getting Things Done* (New York: Crowne Business, 2002).

2. A remark attributed to Peter Drucker and popularized in 2006 by Mark Fields, president of Ford Motor Company.

3. Several YouTube videos capture Marissa Mayer presenting the nine principles to various audiences, or search "Marissa Mayer's 9 Principles of Innovation." A summary by Chuck Salter can be found at http://www.fastcompany.com/702926/marissa-mayers-9-principles-innovation.

4. Steven Johnson, *Where Good Ideas Come From: The Natural History of Innovation* (New York: Riverhead Books, 2010).

5. For a more in-depth conversation about reframing critical conversations, see Gil Rendle, *Journey in the Wilderness: New Life for Mainline Churches* (Nashville: Abingdon Press, 2010), 94–95.

Epilogue

1. "A Covenant Prayer in the Wesleyan Tradition," *The United Methodist Hymnal* (Nashville: The United Methodist Publishing House, 1989), 607. Used by permission.